MW01258386

.d

# Southern California

## PLASTIC SURGERY COOKBOOK

**Kathleen Helen Lisson, CLT**

# Southern California Plastic Surgery Cookbook

By the author of *Plastic Surgery Recovery Handbook*

Recipes for preparing for and recovering from Brazilian butt lift, facelift, liposuction, mommy makeovers and other plastic surgery procedures.

The information provided in this book is not intended as I I specific medical advice. This book is for general informational purposes only and not to replace an individualized treatment plan or physician consultation. The tips discussed in this book were compiled through reviewing research studies and published literature on plastic surgery, interviewing experts, and listening to clients. Experts may disagree and scientific advances may render some of this information outdated. The author assumes no responsibility for any outcome of applying the information in this book for self-care. I am not a nutritionist or dietitian. If you have any safety-related questions about the application of techniques discussed in this book, please consult your physician, plastic surgeon, or registered dietitian.

**ISBN-13: 978-1-7328066-5-8**

# CONTENTS

# Introduction

Kathleen Lisson is dedicated to your successful recovery from plastic surgery. She is moving the bar forward for people who want a holistic approach to post-surgical care. As a massage therapist and certified lymphedema therapist, she has gone out of her way to source information on diet, herbs, spices and enzymes so that you can have a productive discussion with your surgeon about your best post-operative care. When you use her guide to consider your nutrition goals post-surgery and your barriers to success, you will be able to put a plan in place to allow for the best healing experience. Her book is incredibly thorough and will provide you with the tools to need to dip deeper into a number of topics. I recommend you read this book before your surgery to give you time to set up your post-surgery healing kitchen. Her recipe collection includes enticing meals that I'm sure you will enjoy after surgery and for years to come.

Jean LaMantia
jeanlamantia.com
Registered Dietitian and Author of;
*The Essential Cancer Treatment Nutrition Guide and Cookbook*
*The Complete Lymphedema Management and Nutrition Guide The Cancer Risk Reduction Guide*
*Intermittent Fasting; The Complete Guide to Fasting for Your Health, Weight & Wellness*

# CHAPTER 1:
# WHY I WROTE THIS BOOK

The first few chapters focus on nutrition advice and research. If you want to go straight to the kitchen advice and delicious recipes, skip ahead to Chapter 6.

First, let me share why I wrote this book. I was inspired by the stories behind two foods–instant mashed potatoes and Kichadi.

My first experience with eating after surgery happened the week after I shattered my cheekbone in a skiing accident. I was discharged from the hospital after facial reconstruction surgery with instructions to focus on eating foods that were easy to chew and digest.

I felt so excited! I LOVE comfort foods. I imagined sipping vegetable bouillon and eating instant mashed potatoes with butter to my heart's content. I remember wandering around the drug store and looking at the labels of meal replacement drinks for seniors while my prescriptions were being filled. I bought a few of those, too. That was the sum total of my post-surgery nutrition plan.

I had no idea how difficult and tiring it would be to cook. I could barely stand in the shower, let alone the kitchen!

I had no idea how soon it would be until I was sick of instant mashed potatoes.

I had no idea that salty foods increased swelling.

I absolutely had no idea which foods could have helped me reduce inflammation and bring my body back into balance.

If what I ate was a big part of recovering from surgery, someone would have told me, right?

Talk about what NOT to do. Over a decade later, I am so happy to have put the information in this book together to ensure that you do not have to suffer through the same experience.

I shared the mashed potatoes story. What's the part about Kichadi?

In the spring of 2019 a family friend from India ended up in the emergency room and I spent the next few weeks visiting him in the hospital as he recovered. When the nurses were trying to take him off a feeding tube, his first "real" food was thickened yogurt. We all agreed it was disgusting, but it was essential to demonstrate that he could swallow safely. My friend spent the next few days animatedly convincing all his visitors that hospital food sucked and that all he needed was some good, home cooked Indian food.

He was right-once he was discharged, he positively thrived eating the recipes that are commonly served in India when someone is sick. Kichadi, a lentil and rice dish, is known in South India as a dish that is 'good for health.'

Watching him recover made me remember my own recovery more than a decade earlier. Maybe I had not taken my recovery seriously enough, since it was 'just plastic surgery.' I didn't ask any of my friends or coworkers for help. I thought I could do it all on my own and not inconvenience anyone else. In the stress of preparing for the operation, I forgot my own 'good for health' family recipes. Instead, I thought that recovering was a chance to pamper myself. A steady diet of processed foods would make me feel better until I recovered, right? I learned the hard way that the answer to this question was no.

I am so glad my friend was smart enough to put his wellness first.

If I had to do it again, I would plan my meals in advance. Here are a few options:

## Options for Eating After Surgery

- **Cook batches** of entrees and soups before surgery and refrigerate or freeze them
- Enlist **the help of friends and family** to pick up groceries and make meals while you are recovering
- Buy **premade meals** and salads at the deli department of many supermarkets

- Use a **grocery delivery service**-a great option for getting fresh food delivered to your home when you cannot make it to the store
- Try a **meal prep service**. Meal prep services offer premade heat-and-eat meals

But wait, why can't we just grab a few cans of soup and frozen dinners from the supermarket (or finally finish the cans and boxes of food in the back of the cupboard) and take supplements to ensure we're getting enough nutrition? Check with your plastic surgeon—many surgeons ask patients to stop all supplementation for a few weeks before and after surgery. If you feel puffy or bloated after eating certain salty, processed foods before surgery, imagine how horrible you'll feel if you're also swollen from recent liposuction or a facelift.

I wrote this book to be the resource I wish I had before my surgery. I want it to be YOUR resource! I will offer many options for you to add your own tips, preferences, and advice for yourself, including the blank lines below.

How do you want to preplan your meals after surgery? What are your resources?

_____

_____

# CHAPTER 2:

# NUTRITION BEFORE AND AFTER SURGERY

When planning for your upcoming surgery, there are some common pre- and post-surgery issues you need to be aware of and plan for. Let's start with an interview with Registered Dietitian Jean LaMantia and then review other common concerns.

## Interview with Registered Dietitian Jean La Mantia

According to Registered Dietitian Jean LaMantia, what you eat before and after surgery can help with healing. I asked her a few questions about nutrition before and after surgery.

*What are some nutrients we should be looking to incorporate into our daily meals before and after surgery? What does our body need more of when we are healing?*

"The most important nutrients for wound healing (including surgical wounds) are protein, vitamin C and zinc. Consuming dietary sources of these nutrients would be a good strategy to help prepare for surgery."

*Can what we eat affect post-surgery constipation?*

"Many people become constipated after surgery due to the limited mobility as well as the pain medications that can slow down the bowels. You may want to adjust your post-surgery diet for this. For example, you can limit foods known to constipate such as cheese, red meat, and white bread.

You should pay attention to your eating leading up to surgery to get your bowels moving regularly. To do this, there are three key components that you should plan for, which are fiber, fluid, and activity. After surgery, when activity is limited, you may need to include additional soluble fiber in the diet.

Soluble fibers act like a sponge and can help to keep fluid in the stool and keep it from drying out and becoming harder to pass. Straining to have a bowel movement is not recommended as it can put pressure on stitches, especially in the abdominal area. Soluble fibers include oats, chia, and eggplant"

Jean is available for personal consultations. Find out more at https://jeanlamantia.com/

## What else should we watch out for?

### Anemia

Anemia hits close to home for me. Like many women, I have had low blood iron levels my whole life. It had an impact on my high school running and sometimes makes me feel faint as an adult, especially when I'm dehydrated.

Iron plays an important role in correcting anemia and healing. Preoperative anemia affects 30–40 percent of patients undergoing major surgery and is an independent risk factor for perioperative blood transfusion, morbidity, and mortality.

Absolute or functional iron deficiency is its leading cause. If your iron levels are low before surgery you may need 6–8 weeks of supplements to correct this, and that assumes you can tolerate the supplements (Gómez-Ramírez et al. 2019).

In wound healing, iron deficiency results in impaired immune cell function (specifically T cells and phagocytes) in the inflammatory phase and decreased tensile strength and collagen synthesis in the formation of the scar. It can also inhibit wound healing due to decreased oxygen transport to proliferating tissues. (Quain and Khardori 2015).

Some supplements, including turmeric, may inhibit your body's ability to absorb iron (Smith and Ashar 2019). Talk to your plastic surgeon about your iron levels well in advance of your surgery so you have adequate time to make any dietary changes. Iron supplementation may not be a good idea after surgery because of its effect on the gastrointestinal system, including constipation and stomach upset.

According to dietician Caroline Kaufman, iron in foods from

animal sources are more readily absorbed by the body. These include beef, oysters, turkey and dark meat chicken. Iron absorption in foods high in non-heme iron is improved by consuming them with a source of vitamin C. Foods high in non-heme iron include baked potatoes, beans and lentils, cashews, dark green leafy vegetables, tofu, and whole grain breads (Kaufman, 2020).

## Tips for maximizing iron intake:

- Don't consume iron-rich foods with coffee or tea
- Don't consume iron-rich foods with calcium-rich foods
- Do pair non-heme iron-rich foods with vitamin-C-rich foods
- Supplemental iron "is best absorbed when taken on an empty stomach with a full 8-ounce glass of water or orange juice" (Simonson 2019).

What can you do to keep your iron at optimum levels?

_____

_____

## Blood Sugar Control

If you have diabetes, you will need to do extra blood sugar checks in the days and weeks after surgery. The blood sugar could be higher than normal due to the stress on the body or lower than normal due to low food intake and low energy levels. Your blood sugar level will have a direct impact on wound healing. Paying extra attention to keeping your blood sugars in the normal range is very important.Normal fasting blood sugars are 80-130 mg/dl (4-7 mmol/L) and 2 hours after eating: less than 180 mg/dl (10mmol/L).

If you have diabetes, what can you do to make sure your blood sugars are within normal range after surgery?

_____

_____

## Constipation

Most of my clients complain of constipation after surgery. I let them know it's normal and may be from the anesthesia medication. I also remind them that they are moving around less, eating and drinking less and often taking pain killers. All of these contribute to constipation post surgery. Don't strain on the toilet! What you can do to help is drink plenty of fluids, take regular walks (even if they are just inside the home) and include sources of fiber in your diet. But trust me, don't go overboard on the fiber all at once. If you haven't eaten much for a couple of days, be sure to gradually increase your fiber intake.

Foods that are good sources of fiber include beans, chia

seeds, lentils, peas, and raspberries. Prunes and prune juice can be particularly effective. Be sure to drink plenty of water with fiber rich foods. You may want to be sure to have some stool softener medication on hand, these are gentler than laxatives. Don't go more than three days without a bowel movement. If you do, then get in touch with your doctor.

What high fiber foods do you enjoy?

_____

_____

## Inflammation

It is common right after surgery to have inflammation at the site of the procedure. In fact, this is normal and helpful to the body. Signs of inflammation include: redness, heat, pain, swelling and loss of function.

When you have inflammation, it means that the body has called its cellular first responders to come and help it heal. It is a perfectly normal, helpful response to surgery. What isn't helpful is when this short-term (acute) inflammation becomes long term (chronic) inflammation. In fact, this chronic inflammation is a risk factor for diabetes, heart disease, cancer, Alzheimer's and other chronic health conditions.

There is an established anti-inflammatory diet, but

remember the initial inflammation after your surgery is helpful. Inflammation is only a problem if it continues long term. The anti-inflammatory diet is a plant-based diet. The dietary pattern most often studied for this is the traditional Mediterranean diet. There are many books and resources about this popular way of eating. Find information on the Healthy Mediterranean-Style Eating Pattern

here: https://health.gov/our-work/food-nutrition/2015-2020-dietary-guidelines/guidelines/appendix-4/

## Malnutrition

There is something else to watch out for—malnutrition! Some people try to lose as much weight as possible before surgery. If you are cutting calories or fasting, you may be at risk for malnutrition. One big red flag is eating less than 50 percent of your normal diet in the week or weeks before surgery.

Crash dieting either before or after surgery is a bad idea. Your body needs calories and a variety of nutritious foods.

Here are the facts: in "American Society for Enhanced Recovery and Perioperative Quality Initiative Joint Consensus Statement on Nutrition Screening and Therapy Within a Surgical Enhanced Recovery Pathway," Wischmeyer et al. say "it is well known that suboptimal nutritional status is a strong independent predictor of poor postoperative outcomes" and "in surgical patients overall, perioperative nutrition interventions can improve surgical outcomes and reduce infectious morbidity and mortality." The authors state that "preoperative albumin level ... is a predictor of postoperative complications, including morbidity/mortality" (Wischmeyer et al. 2018).

In the article "Evaluation of Malnutrition in Orthopaedic Surgery," Cross et al. explain "obesity and diabetes are common comorbid conditions in patients who are malnourished" and conclude that "preoperative nutrition assessment and optimization of nutritional parameters, including tight glucose control, normalization of serum albumin, and safe weight loss, may reduce the risk of perioperative complications, including infection" (Cross et al. 2014). Crash diets and restricting calories are never a safe way to change your weight.

Your size and body weight are not a good indicator of malnutrition. Even if you are in a larger body, you can still be deficient in important vitamins and/or minerals. This is more of a risk if you don't eat a wide enough variety of foods–especially if you eliminate an entire food group from your diet! Foods are actually organized into the traditional food groups because they have similar vitamins and minerals. For example, foods in the grain group are good sources of fiber and B vitamins. Fruits and vegetables are good sources of vitamin C, Vitamin A, and folate. If you eliminate an entire group, your risk of malnutrition is higher.

In addition to vitamins and minerals, protein requirements are elevated in times of stress, and this includes surgery, even elective cosmetic surgery. It's important to achieve an even distribution of protein throughout your day. To achieve this, include protein at each of your meals and snacks (Wischmeyer et al. 2018).

## Are You Eating Enough Calories?

The Body Weight Planner at www.niddk.nih.gov/bwp can help calculate daily caloric needs for maintaining weight.

## Nausea

Everyone reacts differently to surgical anesthesia, and you may find yourself feeling nauseated after surgery. If this is the case, try to rely on cold or room-temperature foods. They have less aroma than hot foods, and it's the aroma that may trigger the nausea. This may mean that if there are others in the house, they may need to cook while you are sleeping. Be sure to use the kitchen exhaust fan.

If you feel nauseated, try a smoothie. Keep the lid on the container and drink through a straw. Taking small sips throughout the day and not letting your stomach get empty can help, too. Ginger can help for some forms of nausea. You may like to nibble on ginger snap cookies or sip on cold ginger tea or ginger ale.

Tips that I would like to try to reduce nausea:

_____

_____


## Probiotics, Synbiotics and Surgical Site Infections

A systematic review and analysis of randomized controlled trials in 2015 found that probiotics and synbiotics in adult patients undergoing elective abdominal surgery reduce the risk of surgical site infections compared to placebo or standard of care (Lytvyn et al. 2015).

### What are probiotics?

Probiotics are live helpful bacteria. They are contained in certain foods and may help your digestive wellness. Probiotics have been used to improve human health by influencing the type and amount of bacteria living in your intestines, called your microbiota.

### What are prebiotics?

Prebiotics are fibers that are indigestible to us, but are beneficial to our microbiota.

### What are synbiotics?

"Synbiotics" is the term used to describe the synergistic effect of probiotics and prebiotics working together. Synergistic means a combined effect that is better than two separate effects added together. Synbiotics would be prebiotics (fiber) and probiotics (live bacteria) working together.

In addition to protection from infection, the gut microbiota regulates inflammation (Illiani et al 2020). Many things can influence the type and amount of your microbiota, including your history of bacterial infections, antibiotic treatment, lifestyle, surgery, and diet.

In his book *Eat to Heal*, Dr. Joseph F. McCaffrey (2017) recommends that his clients "take yogurt and/or probiotics twice a day whenever you're on antibiotics and for at least a couple of weeks afterwards. Take the probiotics with meals, and don't take them at the same time as the antibiotics."

## Let's learn more about probiotics

Simply put, a probiotic is a food made with lactic acid fermentation and consumed raw. Markowiak and Śliżewska (2017) say "the introduction of probiotics, prebiotics, or synbiotics into human diet is favourable for the intestinal microbiota. They may be consumed in the form of raw vegetables and fruit, fermented pickles, or dairy products."

Examples of probiotics that can be found at most supermarkets include buttermilk, kefir, sauerkraut, and pickles. Kimchi is another example, and Patra et al. (2016) mention that "different types of fermented foods such as chongkukjang, doenjang, ganjang, gochujang, and kimchi are plentifully available and widely consumed in north eastern Asian countries including Korea." The researchers say "kimchi possesses anti-inflammatory, antibacterial, antioxidant, anticancer, antiobesity, probiotic, cholesterol lowering and antiaging properties."

I am part German and remember my grandmother serving sauerkraut at holiday meals. My husband is from India and we eat probiotic yogurt alongside Indian meals. For example, raita is a dish combining yogurt with diced cucumber, green onions, cilantro and coriander.

## Prebiotics

Prebiotics are fiber that helps nourish the bacteria in your gut. Prebiotic fibers have been shown to help your immune function, and this could help you fight infection.

Which foods are prebiotic? Markowiak and Śliżewska (2017) state that prebiotics include "tomatoes, artichokes, bananas, asparagus, berries, garlic, onions, chicory, green vegetables, legumes, as well as oats, linseed, barley, and wheat" but caution that "an overdose of prebiotics may lead to flatulence and diarrhoea."

Monash University has tips on prebiotics for those following a low FODMAP diet here: www.monashfodmap.com/blog/dietary-fibre-series-prebiotic-fibre/

Which probiotics and prebiotics do you like to eat? Do you have family recipes that include probiotics or prebiotics?

_____

_____

## Protein (Albumin)

In addition to probiotics, prebiotics and synbiotics, protein can also play a role in reducing surgical site infection. Researchers looked at more than 49,000 orthopedic surgery patients and found that, in comparison to patients with normal albumin concentration, patients with low blood albumin levels had a higher risk for surgical site infection, pneumonia, extended length of stay in the hospital, and readmission (Bohl et al. 2016).

### What is albumin?

Albumin is a protein made by your liver that keeps fluid from leaking out of your bloodstream into other tissues. Sometimes, low albumin levels are a result of a diet too low in protein. Low albumin levels may also be a warning sign of illness.

## Nerve Recovery

Most of my clients complain of numbness after surgery, followed by tingling sensations in the months afterwards.

I reassure them that's a completely normal part of the healing process.

## Can eating foods containing B vitamins help nerves regenerate?

Turkish researchers from Kahramanmaras Sutcu Imam University state "vitamin B complex helps to alleviate degeneration in the nervous system and . . . these vitamins, in particular vitamin B12, exhibit important roles in various biological events to maintain normal neural functions" and found that "tissue levels of vitamin B complex and vitamin B12 vary with progression of crush-induced peripheral nerve injury, and supplementation of these vitamins in the acute period may be beneficial for acceleration of nerve regeneration" (Altun and Kurutaş 2016). Foods rich in B vitamins include meats and fish like salmon and trout, leafy greens, legumes, nutritional yeast, and yogurt.

Which B vitamin-rich foods do you enjoy eating?

_____

_____


## Postoperative Ileus (a.k.a Help, I can't poop!)

Postoperative ileus is a temporary condition where the bowels are unable to function, so they can't move feces out of the body. This can happen after surgery.

## Chewing gum

According to a study published in Digestive Surgery, researchers found that chewing gum shows a favorable effect on the time elapsed before passing gas and having a bowel movement. If your surgeon allows you to chew gum after your surgery, the act of chewing may reactivate your digestive system (de Castro et al. 2008).

## Drinking coffee or tea

According to the study "Effect of Caffeine Intake on Postoperative Ileus: A Systematic Review and Meta-Analysis," researchers found "drinking coffee after surgery improves bowel motility and reduces the time to first bowel movement (and) the time to first passing gas" (Gkegkes et al. 2019).

What is your favorite type of coffee, tea or chewing gum?

_____

_____

# Supplements and Medications

'Wait a second,' you might be thinking. 'Why is it important to consume a nutritious diet BEFORE surgery? My doctor actually told me to STOP taking my supplements.'

Your plastic surgeon is right! Some supplements that are normally beneficial for us can actually be harmful when combined with a surgical procedure. Want to know more? Read the article "Herbal Medicines and Perioperative Care" at www.hopkinsmedicine.org/gim/_pdf/consult/herbal_meds.pdf

## Make sure your medications aren't putting you at risk

If you take prescription medications regularly or will be taking pain medications, contact your pharmacist and ask them to review your medications for any potential risk of drug-induced nutrient depletion or drug / supplement interactions. Read more about potential interactions at the website of the American Academy of Family Physicians: www.aafp.org/dam/AAFP/documents/about_us/sponsored_resources/Nature%20Made%20Handout.pdf

## Wound Healing

When you have surgery, there will be a wound that needs to heal afterwards. Nutrition plays a key role in wound healing and impacts how well you recover. Three key nutrients involved in wound healing are protein, vitamin C, and zinc.

## Let's talk protein!

Protein intake is important after surgery to maintain lean body mass (LBM). In the article "Nutrition in Wound Care Management: A Comprehensive Overview," Quain and Khardori (2015) state that "the presence of a wound increases protein demand by up to 250% and caloric demand by up to 50% to maintain adequate LBM stores. Depletion of 10% of LBM is associated with impaired immunity and risk of infection." They also mention that "amino acids have also been implicated in the role of wound healing" and describe the role of vitamins A, C, and D in wound healing.

What types of protein do you like?

_____

_____

Why exactly is protein important? In the article "Nutrition and the Plastic Surgeon: Possible Interventions and Practice Considerations," published in *Plastic and Reconstructive Surgery - Global Open*, Roy et al. (2018) state that "up to 25% of plastic surgery outpatients are at risk for malnutrition" and mention a similar list of nutrients. They also explain that "protein depletion leads to a prolonged inflammatory phase by decreasing fibroblast proliferation, proteoglycan synthesis, and neoangiogenesis."

## Other vitamins that support wound healing

Roy et al. (2018) go on to state that "micronutrients also play significant roles in the process of wound healing. Vitamin A stimulates fibroblasts, vitamin C promotes collagen synthesis and fibroblast proliferation and zinc is essential for protein and collagen synthesis."

Vitamin D is also important for wound healing. Yuan et al. found that "vitamin D has a positive effect on diabetes-impaired wounds. The improved wound healing is associated with reduced inflammation in diabetic wounds" (Yuan et al., 2018). Vitamin D deficiency may also play a role in several types of fibrosis in the body (Can Vitamin D Tame Fibrosis?, 2013).

The Cleveland Clinic published "Nutrition Guidelines to Improve Wound Healing." View it here: my.clevelandclinic.org/health/articles/11111-nutrition-guidelines-to-improve-wound-healing

Alberta Health Services published "Eating Well for Wound Healing" with lists of suggested foods here: www.albertahealthservices.ca/assets/info/nutrition/if-nfs-eatig-well-for-wound-healing.pdf

# CHAPTER 3:

# PLANT A RECOVERY GARDEN (OR SHOP IN THE PRODUCE SECTION)

I live in a condominium and enjoy growing herbs on my balcony. I can wake up in the morning and enjoy a cup of fresh tea by adding a few leaves of mint to a cup of hot water from the kettle. I add fresh spices and garnishes to soups, salads and stir fry dishes.

Can you grow a small herb and spice garden that will help you prepare tasty, fresh, nutritious foods both before and after surgery?

## HERBS

What are some herbs you could grow?

**Aloe Vera** (Aloe vera) has been traditionally grown for the inner gel from the fresh leaf. Cut it off near the inner stalk, removing spines and splitting lengthwise. Topical skin sensitization may occur. People allergic to garlic, onions, and tulips may be allergic to aloe.

**Basil** (Ocimum basilicum) contains 1,8-Cineole,

a monoterpene oxide that is anti-inflammatory (Kunnumakkara, 2018). Fresh basil should be added to dishes at the end of cooking. Torres (2006) says that "basil leaves and sometimes the flowering tips of the plant are used, either fresh or dry, to make a tea."

**Calendula** (Calendula officinalis) has traditionally been used for tissue inflammation and wounded tissues. The flower petals can be added to recipes or used in a tea.

**Chamomile** (Chamaemelum nobile) is traditionally used as a sleep aid and to balance digestion. Torres (2006) states that "those who wish to break the nicotine habit should chew fresh or dried chamomile flowers when the urge for a cigarette strikes." To prepare a tea, use 1-3 grams of flowers steeped in eight ounces of hot water for ten minutes. Avoid if allergic to the ragweed or daisy family. It's also best to avoid chamomile if you are on blood thinner medication.

**Cleavers** (Galium aparine) "is one of numerous plants considered in ancient times to act as a diuretic. It was therefore used to relieve edema" (Cleavers, 2015).

**Echinacea** (Echinacea angustifolia) is traditionally used as a tea during cold and flu season. It's best to avoid echinacea if you are on blood thinner medication or immunosuppressants. Don't consume echinacea before surgery.

**Gotu kola** (Centella asiatica) is used culinarily in several parts of Asia. In the article, "Antifibrotic Herbs: Indications, Mechanisms of Action, Doses, and Safety Information," Yarnell and Abascal (2013) state that gotu kola is an "herb of great utility, including use as an antifibrotic" and mentioned "two other preliminary clinical trials found that crude extracts of gotu kola prevented formation of postsurgical adhesions and reduced postsurgical scarring."

**Holy basil**. See **Tulsi**.

**Lavender** (Lavandula angustifolia) has been traditionally used in cooking or as a tea to settle the stomach. According to the National Center for Complementary and Integrative Health (NCCIH 2016), "lavender has a long history of use to boost appetite and mood, as well as relieve gastrointestinal problems and anxiety" and "people may also inhale a lavender vapor to help sleep, (and) to reduce pain." Torres (2006) says "the flowers are brewed into a tea and taken as a sedative" and "a few drops of essence of lavender on the forehead will cure headaches." Use ½ tablespoon per cup of water for tea and steep for at least three minutes (NCCIH, 2016).

**Lemon balm** (Melissa officinalis) has been traditionally used to reduce stress, ease mild anxiety, and reduce stomach upset. Take ¼–1 teaspoon of dried leaves in 8 ounces of hot water or use freshly chopped leaves from the garden. Scallan (2003) recommends chopping leaves "finely and sprinkling on fruit salad" and comments that "it tastes good in egg dishes, especially omelettes, and goes well with vegetables of all kinds." Best to avoid lemon balm if you are taking diabetes or thyroid medications.

**Marshmallow Root** (Althaea officinalis) has been traditionally used to decrease inflammation by forming a barrier against irritants such as stomach acid. Demulcent (anti-inflammatory) herbs should be taken far apart (a few hours at least) from any medications. Try marshmallow as a macerate (softened/steeped herb; see Chapter 5 for more information on macerates), but be wary of potential interactions with diabetes drugs and anticoagulants. Note that marshmallow is no longer an ingredient in modern recipes for the fluffy sweet treat of the same name.

**Oregano** (Origanum vulgare) has been traditionally used for its antifungal and antibacterial properties. It is used widely as a culinary herb.

**Parsley** (Petroselinum crispum) has been traditionally used to balance digestion and kidney function. It is often used as a garnish and can be added to smoothies. Scallan (2003) says that "the stalks of the parsley are more strongly flavoured than the leaves and are used in stock pots and stews. The leaves can garnish all manner of vegetable and savoury dishes." Torres (2006) states that "an infusion of fresh leaves makes a tea that is used to relieve indigestion."

**Passionflower** (Passiflora incarnata) has been traditionally used to help reduce stress and ease mild anxiety. For tea, take 1 teaspoon of dried passionflower or 1 tablespoon of fresh flowers per cup of water. Let the tea steep for about 5 minutes. Limit to one cup per day. It is best to avoid passionflower if you are taking anti-anxiety or anti-depression medication.

**Peppermint** (Mentha piperita) can be used as a culinary ingredient and as a tea or macerate (see Chapter 5 for more on macerates).

McKay and Blumberg (2006) state that "the phenolic constituents of the leaves include rosmarinic acid and several flavonoids, primarily eriocitrin, luteolin and hesperidin. The main volatile components of the essential oil are menthol and menthone. In vitro, peppermint has significant antimicrobial and antiviral activities, strong antioxidant and antitumor actions, and some antiallergenic potential." In addition, peppermint oil may be helpful in reducing nausea. A study by Briggs et al. (2016) showed that "peppermint oil inhalation is a viable first-line treatment for nausea in postoperative cardiac surgery patients." Combine two cups of water and a handful of torn leaves. Using cool water will help preserve the peppermint oils in the leaves. Peppermint oil may interact with cyclosporine, statins, proton pump inhibitors (PPIs), and nonsteroidal anti-inflammatory drugs (NSAIDS).

**Red clover** (Trifolium pratense) can be used as a tea.

According to the Milton S. Hershey Medical Center website, "health care practitioners believe that red clover 'purified' the blood by acting as a diuretic [and] dried herb (used for tea): 1 to 2 tsp dried flowers or flowering tops steeped in 8 oz. hot water for 1/2 hour; drink 2 to 3 cups daily" (Red Clover, 2015). It's best to avoid red clover if you are on blood thinner medication or receiving treatment for estrogen receptor positive breast cancer.

**Rosemary** (Salvia rosmarinus) contains α-Pinene, a monoterpene which "is known to possess antimicrobial, apoptotic, antimetastatic, and antibiotic properties" according to Kunnumakkara et al. (2018). Use a fresh sprig of rosemary steeped for 3-5 minutes in hot water or one teaspoon dried rosemary per cup of boiling water. Torres states that "the leaves are used often to make a tea to aid digestion" (Torres, 2006). Rosemary can also be used to flavor food. Scallan (2003) recommends that you "chop the leaves and include them in vegetable dishes; they are especially effective with peas, potatoes and marrows. They make a distinctive contribution to the flavour of soups and stews."

**Tulsi, or holy basil** (Ocimum sanctum) is used by several cultures. Jamshidi and Cohen (2017) found that "the most commonly used part of the tulsi plant is the leaf (dried or fresh), which is known to contain several bioactive compounds including eugenol, ursolic acid, β-caryophyllene, linalool, and 1,8-cineole." They also stated that "the findings from 24 human studies published to date suggest that the tulsi is a safe herbal intervention that may assist in normalising glucose, blood pressure and lipid profiles, and dealing with psychological and immunological stress. Furthermore, these studies indicate the daily addition of tulsi to the diet and/or as adjunct to drug therapy can potentially assist in prevention or reduction of various health conditions." Fresh tea can be made from the flowers on the top few inches of the plant.

Plants I Would Like To Grow in my Garden

_____

_____

NOTE: I am not a dietitian, herbalist or nutritionist. If you would like to know more about herbs, consider booking an appointment with an herbalist. Here are some of my recommendations:

Southern California Herbalist Shana Lipner Grover, sagecountryherbs.com

Southern California Herbalist Julie James, greenwisdomherbalstudies.com

South Carolina Herbalist Angelina Shuman, wildearthherbals.com

# FRUITS

Let's look at a few delicious and nutritious fruits to add to our grocery list.

**Cantaloupe and Citrus fruits**. Cantaloupe and many citrus fruits contain Vitamin C. McCaffrey (2011) states that "vitamin C is crucial for wound healing and scar formation." Vitamin C has been shown to increase iron absorption.

**Chili peppers** (Capsicum annuum) are a fruit! According to Kunnumakkara et al. (2018), "capsaicin (trans-8-methyl-N-vanillyl6-nonenamide) is a principal component of the spice red pepper (Capsicum)" and "studies revealed that capsaicin inhibits inflammatory cytokines." Use in cooking to add spice to your dishes.

**Kiwifruit** (Actinidia deliciosa) are a delicious fruit that may go well with meals. Some people may find different types of protein-rich foods like yogurt, cheese, and fish difficult to digest. In the article "Influence of Kiwifruit on Protein Digestion," published in Advances in Food and Nutrition Research, Kaur and Boyland (2013) say "Green kiwifruit consumption has long been thought to assist in the digestion of food proteins due to the presence of the proteolytic enzyme actinidin" and that "clear evidence is provided that green kiwifruit, and the enzyme actinidin itself, can provide enhanced upper-tract digestion (particularly gastric) of a variety of food proteins, which lends support to a role for dietary kiwifruit as a digestive aid."

**Papaya** (Carica papaya L.) is a tropical fruit grown in several countries including the United States, India, and Mexico. Muss, Mosgoeller and Endler (2013) found that "ingredients of the papaya fruit (Carica papaya L.) and the processed fruit have been associated with beneficial impact on digestion or diseases" and "the fruit is considered a traditional remedy for gastrointestinal functional disorders in countries with papaya plants."

**Pineapple** (Ananas comosus) stems contain bromelain. Orsini (2007) states that "bromelain may be of particular interest in plastic surgery because of its apparent antiedematous, anti-inflammatory, and anticoagulation properties. Additional evidence suggests that bromelain may be beneficial in pain reduction, wound healing, burn debridement, and ischemia/reperfusion" (Muhammad & Ahmad, 2017).

Boiling has been traditionally used to extract the bromelain from the pineapple skin. Use organic pineapples and place skins in a cooking pot. Cover with water and boil for 10 minutes. Turn heat down and simmer for 45 minutes. Strain and save the liquid. Make sure that adding bromelain does not interfere with prescription medication you are taking, including antibiotics and anticoagulants: www.mskcc.org/cancer-care/integrative-medicine/herbs/bromelain

Eating fruits and a wide range of vegetables is a delicious way to add nutrients to your diet!

Fruits I Would Like to Try

_____

_____

## ROOTS, RHIZOMES AND THE DRIED SPICE SHELF

**Black Pepper** (Piper nigrum) is a common spice. According to Kunnumakkara et al. (2018), "piperine is the principal plant alkaloid isolated from black pepper (Piper nigrum) and long pepper (Piper longum). Piperine has several biological properties including analgesic, anti-convulsant, anti-tumor and anti-inflammatory activities."

**Cinnamon** (Cinnamomum zeylanicum) is a delicious spice derived from the bark of the cinnamon tree. "Cinnamaldehyde (CM) is the active component of the spice cinnamon (Cinnamomum zeylanicum). This component is widely known for its anti-inflammatory, antimicrobial, anti-oxidant, anti-tumor, cholesterol lowering and immunomodulatory properties" according to Kunnumakkara et al. (2018). Cinnamon tea can be made from powder or cinnamon sticks.

**Dandelion** (Taraxacum officinale) root has been traditionally used in tea as a diuretic. It is best to avoid dandelion if you are allergic to ragweed, daisies, chrysanthemums, or marigolds.

**Garlic** (Allium sativum) is a delicious culinary ingredient. According to Kunnumakkara et al. (2018), garlic "possesses anti-inflammatory, gastroprotective and anti-cancer properties." Torres (2006) says garlic should be used fresh and adds "there is no question that garlic has antibacterial and anti-inflammatory properties." McCaffrey (2011) recommends chopping garlic and letting it "sit for five minutes before cooking." Don't consume in the days before surgery and ask your surgeon for specific advice on when to stop consuming garlic and other ingredients that may increase your risk of bleeding.

**Ginger root** (Zingiber officinale) contains the protease zingibain as well as gingerols. According to Kunnumakkara et al. (2018), "6-Gingerol, the main active component of ginger, is shown to possess different biological activities such as anti-oxidative, anti-inflammatory and anti-proliferative properties." Ginger tea has been traditionally used for nausea. It may cause stomach upset if taken on an empty stomach and is best avoided by any person who is on blood thinner medication. Ginger root can also be thinly sliced and added to smoothies or juiced.

**Onions** (Allium cepa) are commonly used as a culinary ingredient. According to Kunnumakkara et al. (2018), "quercetin is a dietary flavonoid obtained from onions. The anti-cancer, anti-inflammatory, and antioxidant properties of this phytochemical are demonstrated by numerous studies." If you are worried about preparing raw onions, many grocery stores sell pre sliced onions. McCaffrey (2011) recommends chopping onions and letting them sit for a few minutes before cooking.

**Turmeric** (Curcuma longa) is used for the root. Kunnumakkara et al. (2018) say "this 'golden spice' is recognized for its anti-inflammatory, antimicrobial, insecticidal, antimutagenic, radioprotective, and anticancer properties." Kim et al. (2009) state that "curcumin, the bioactive component of curry spice turmeric, and its related structures possess potent anti-oxidant and anti-inflammatory properties" and that "curcuminoids increased the phosphorylation of AMP-activated protein kinase (AMPK)." Please choose fresh turmeric from the grocery store instead of powdered as powdered can sometimes include additives used to increase the color intensity.

## More spices for balancing inflammation

Can you make the recipes you love with a pinch or two of extra spices? The University of Wisconsin Integrative Health recommends the spices "paprika, rosemary, ginger, turmeric, sage, cumin, cloves, Jamaican allspice, cinnamon, marjoram, [and] tarragon" to reduce inflammation. Read the article "Anti Inflammatory Lifestyle" at www.fammed.wisc.edu/files/webfm-uploads/documents/outreach/im/handout_ai_diet_patient.pdf

In the article "Chronic diseases, inflammation, and spices: how are they linked?" Kunnumakkara et al. (2018) say "tremendous studies have shown that nutraceuticals derived from spices such as clove, coriander, garlic, ginger, onion, pepper, turmeric, etc., remarkably prevent and cure various chronic diseases by targeting inflammatory pathways."

Spices and Roots I Would Like to Try

_____

_____

# CHAPTER 4:
## ENZYMES

We have added fruits, spices and herbs to our shopping list. What about enzymes? Learning about enzymes was the most exciting part of researching this book. As with all dietary supplements, manufacturers are exempt from having to prove that their product is safe or it works as long as they don't claim that they diagnose, treat, cure or prevent any disease.

## What Are Enzymes?

Enzymes are proteins that help the body perform chemical reactions. They act as catalysts, meaning that they speed up reactions. There are many types, but I will first focus on digestive enzymes.

You may be familiar with digestive enzymes. These enzymes are made and secreted in the digestive tract to help you digest your meal.

Natural digestive enzymes that your body produces include:

- Lingual lipase
- Salivary amylase
- Gastric lipase
- Pepsin

- Lactase
- Sucrase

You can also take enzymes as a supplement. There are two main types: a prescription digestive enzyme and over-the-counter. The prescription version is sometimes prescribed to treat diseases including cystic fibrosis, pancreatitis, or pancreatic cancer. It is an enteric-coated tablet containing amylase, lipase, and protease to help your body digest carbohydrate, fat, and protein, respectively (Harvard, 2020).

## Proteolytic enzymes

Proteolytic enzymes, sometimes called protease, proteinase, or peptidase, are enzymes that break proteins, including fibrin, a protein involved in forming blood clots, into amino acids. Proteolytic enzyme treatments were first used in Germany in the 1960s for inflammation, osteoarthritis, autoimmune diseases, and viral infections. The products usually contain a mixture of pancreatin, papain, bromelain, trypsin, and chymotrypsin (Proteolytic Enzymes, 2019).

Plant proteases such as bromelain, ficin and papain are widely used in the food industry for various applications such as brewing, tenderization of meat, coagulation of milk and as a digestive aid (Raveendran et al. 2018). Eating these enzymes with food will allow them to target the digestive system and eating them on an empty stomach may allow them to pass into the bloodstream.

As mentioned before, bromelain and papain are two proteolytic enzymes. Bromelain is found in pineapple and papain is found in papaya. Does this sound a little familiar? That's because many plastic surgeons will recommend bromelain after surgery.

A brief outline of common protein digesting enzymes

| Name | Origin |
| --- | --- |
| Bromelain | Pineapple stem, fruit and juice |
| Chymotrypsin | Animal pancreas |
| Papain | Papaya |
| Serratiopeptidase | Bacteria |
| Trypsin | Bacteria, fungus or pork |

What do we know about the effect of taking bromelain after surgery? In a study of forty patients undergoing a septoplasty (a procedure to straighten the septum of the nose to allow for improved air passage),researchers looked at the effectiveness of enzymes post-surgery.

In this study, twenty patients in the control group received an anti-inflammatory and a pain reliever. The other twenty patients received an enzyme preparation containing bromelain, trypsin and rutoside. Bromelain and trypsin are both protein-digesting enzymes and rutoside is an anti-inflammatory found in citrus fruit. The authors concluded that the use of oral enzymes in post-operative patients would probably be beneficial (Nanda, 2014).

*"Bromelain thins the blood and could increase risk of bleeding during or after surgery. For this reason, physician supervision is essential."*

In a safety and efficacy report in the journal Plastic and Reconstructive Surgery, Dr. Roger Orsini (2006) summarized the research on the pineapple enzyme bromelain. He advised that it is generally considered safe, in studies in which a dose of 500–1500 mg per day is used.

There is some limited evidence that bromelain may help with pain, edema, inflammation, clotting and antibiotics, but Orsini pointed out that more research is needed. If you choose to use bromelain, be sure to consult your physician about your plan.

In rare cases, bromelain and mixtures containing bromelain may cause nausea, vomiting, diarrhea, allergic reactions, and unusual menstrual bleeding.

*"For enzyme supplements to be effective, the intact enzyme must reach the joints or muscle tissue after absorption from the gastrointestinal tract. To accomplish this, enzymes must be enterically coated or supplemented with a proton pump inhibitor or histamine blocker, to survive passage through the acidic environment of the stomach (Varayil et al. 2014)."*

**Serratiopeptidase** (Serrapeptase)

There is no direct evidence that serratiopeptidase can help healing after plastic surgery, but many people consider taking it during their recovery, so I wanted to present the information I know about this supplement here.

In the article "Serratiopeptidase: a systematic review of the existing evidence," published in the *International Journal of Surgery*, Bhagat et al. state that the proteolytic enzyme "has been used for almost 40 years in Japan and Europe for pain and inflammation." They explain that "serratiopeptidase reduces swelling by the process of decreasing the amount of fluid in the tissues, thinning the fluid, and by facilitating the drainage of fluid. In addition, its enzyme activity dissolves dead tissue surrounding the injured area so that healing is accelerated." It can also "alleviate pain and acts by breaking down fibrin and other dead or damaged tissue without harming living tissue" (Bhagat et al. 2013).

Can an oral dose actually get past the digestive system? It is usually taken on an empty stomach and a study in rats found that "serratiopeptidase is absorbed from the intestine, distributed to the inflammatory site via blood or lymph. Thus, indicating that orally administered serratiopeptidase is absorbed from intestinal tract and reaches circulation in an enzymatically active form" (Bhagat et al. 2013).

Will your plastic surgeon know about this supplement? Bhagat et al. state that "serratiopeptidase is a proteolytic enzyme prescribed in various specialties like surgery, orthopaedics, otorhinolaryngology, gynaecology and dentistry for its anti-inflammatory, anti-edemic and analgesic effects." The authors concluded that "more well-designed, active comparator controlled trials are needed to clearly define the beneficial effects of this natural enzyme claiming to possess miraculous properties" (Bhagat et al. 2013).

## AMPK

I loved learning about AMPK because it is one more reason to keep up our healthy habits before and after surgery. What's the big deal? Let's find out.

Adenosine monophosphate activated protein kinase (AMPK) is an enzyme present in our cells that regulates homeostasis.

Jiang et. al. state that "fibrosis is a common process characterized by excessive extracellular matrix (ECM) accumulation after inflammatory injury, which is also a crucial cause of aging" and that "5'-AMP-activated protein kinase (AMPK) is a pivotal energy sensor that alleviates or delays the process of fibrogenesis" (Jiang et al., 2017).

Fibrosis can be reversed. In the article "Extracellular matrix as a driver of progressive fibrosis," published in *The Journal of Clinical Investigation*, Herrera et al. (2018) state that "when fibroproliferation ensues after a single discrete injury, the process can be reversible or result in a durable scar comprising highly cross-linked collagens and other extracellular matrix (ECM) components."

Why does AMPK work? Jiang et al. explain that "fibrosis is a dynamic response composed of three closely connected processes, including primary inflammatory injury, regulation of effector cells, and ECM secretion. AMPK is a pivotal molecule that prevents or delays the process of fibrogenesis. AMPK exerts comprehensive protective effects against fibrosis in various organs and tissues, including heart, liver, kidney, lung, etc." (Jiang et al., 2017).

How can we help activate AMPK? Kim et al. state that "numerous polyphenols are capable of activating AMPK. These include resveratrol from red grapes, quercetin from many plant units including fruits, vegetables and grains, genistein found in a number of plants such as soybeans, epigallocatechin gallate from green tea, berberine from Coptis chinensis and curcumim from Curcuma longa." Curcuma longa is the scientific name for turmeric. Ginseng (Panax ginseng) and α-Lipoic acid (ALA) are also mentioned (Kim et al., 2016).

## What else works?

Liu et al. (2019) found that omega-3 fatty acids-enriched fish oil "could also significantly activate adenosine monophosphate (AMP)-activated protein kinase (AMPK) phosphorylation."

Another major player in activating AMPK is exercise. Herzig and Shaw (2018) found that "exercise is also a potent activator of AMPK." In the article 'AMPK and the biochemistry of exercise: Implications for human health and disease,' Richter and Ruderman (2009) state that "exercise is perhaps the most powerful physiological activator of AMPK" and that "regular exercise leads to decreased inflammation and increased fibrinolytic activity."

Consuming fruits and vegetables, green tea, omega-3 fatty acids and taking exercise can all increase AMPK–this sounds a lot like the advice we get for a healthy lifestyle already.

## Why is fibrinolytic activity important?

According to Földi and Földi, when acute inflammation is resolved, the "lion's share of the waste disposal is provided by the lymph vessels" and "fibrinolytic enzymes dismantle the fibrin precipitates into building blocks, and these are likewise removed through lymph vessels." What goes wrong? "If the fibrin precipitate is not completely removed, i.e., if fibrin remains in the area of an acute inflammation, the result is fibrosis ... ultimately resulting in fibrosclerosis and scarring" (Földi and Földi, 2012, 360).

# Hormones

Let's learn about the hormone Adiponectin, one of AMPK's best friends!

As someone who works to reduce fibrosis in my clients, you can imagine how excited I got when I saw the title of the following study. In the article "The adipokine adiponectin has potent anti-fibrotic effects mediated via adenosine monophosphate-activated protein kinase: novel target for fibrosis therapy" published in *Arthritis Research & Therapy*, Fang et al. (2012) state that "adiponectin is an adipocyte-derive pleiotropic hormone" and found that it "acts as a potent anti-fibrotic signal."

Fang et al. explain that "adiponectin responses are mediated via AMP kinase, a fuel-sensing cellular enzyme that is necessary and sufficient for down-regulation of fibrotic genes" and state that "adiponectin/AMP kinase pathway may play a previously unrecognized important homeostatic role in ECM [extracellular matrix] regulation, and its defective function contributes to aberrant fibroblast activation in the pathogenesis of fibrosis." The authors say "the inhibitory effects of adiponectin on fibrotic responses were associated with activation of AMP kinase, a stress-induced metabolic master switch that plays a key role in maintaining energy homeostasis" (Fang et al, 2012).

How can we help increase adiponectin? In the article "Specific dietary patterns and concentrations of adiponectin,"

Izadi and Azadbakht state that "lifestyle related factors like physical activity and diet play the important roles on adiponectin." They state that the Mediterranean Diet is helpful for increasing levels of adiponectin because "plasma adiponectin level was 23% higher in women who followed this dietary pattern" with one caveat - they had to be nonsmokers. They list other studies that found that adiponectin increased among people with a "high consumption of low-fat dairy products, whole grain cereals as well as low consumption of refined grains," a "low glycemic index diet with high amount of fiber," as well as unsaturated fats and fruit and vegetable intake (Izadi and Azadbakht, 2015).

Exercise also affects adiponectin levels. In the article "Exercise Increases Adiponectin and Reduces Leptin Levels in Prediabetic and Diabetic Individuals: Systematic Review and Meta-Analysis of Randomized Controlled Trials," published in Medical Sciences, Becic et al. say that "physical exercise and, specifically, aerobic exercise, leads to higher adiponectin and lower leptin levels in prediabetic and diabetic adults" (Becic, 2018).

Be sure to discuss these ideas and any diet change, exercise program or supplement usage with your plastic surgeon.

# CHAPTER 5:
# RECOVERY WATERS AND TEAS

## How can we prepare herbs with water?

There are several ways to prepare herbs with water, including:

Infusion–this preparation works well for flowers, leaves, and roots. One method is to pour 1 cup of near-boiling water over 1–3 teaspoons herb and allow to steep 5–10 minutes.

Macerate–this preparation works well for flowers, leaves, and roots. One method is to pour 1 cup cold or room temperature water over 1-3 teaspoons of herb and allow to steep 1–8 hours. This is preferred if the drinker is not immunocompromised and the herbs have mucilage and/ or volatile oils.

Decoction–this preparation is preferred for dried, hard plant parts like bark or roots. One method is to steep 4 cups room temperature water and 1 oz. of herb for 1 hour, then bring to boil, reduce heat and simmer 10–30 minutes. Strain.

Compress/fomentation–can be made by soaking a cloth in either an infusion or decoction of herbs. Use with cold liquid for acute swelling or warm liquid for soothing muscles.

*TIP: Do not use aluminum or teflon when preparing herbs. Glass is best. (Torres, 2006).*

## Recovery waters

Sometimes it's hard to remember to drink enough water after surgery. Flavorful waters may help! Pour water into a pitcher and add these tasty items:

### PINEAPPLE CINNAMON WATER

1 cup frozen pineapple

1 cinnamon stick

### SPICY WATER

1 teaspoon grated ginger

Sliced cucumber

Sliced Lemon

12 mint leaves

Your favorite flavored water recipes

_____

_____

# Infusions and Macerates

## Infusions

You've just read about these herbs earlier in the book. Which ones would you try in an infusion?

Basil *(Ocimum basilicum)*

Calendula *(Calendula officinalis)*

Chamomile *(Chamaemelum nobile)*

Cinnamon *(Cinnamomum zeylanicum)*

Dandelion *(Taraxacum officinale)*

Ginger *(Zingiber officinale)*

Echinacea *(Echinacea angustifolia)* — Don't drink before surgery

Lavender *(Lavandula angustifolia)*

Lemon balm *(Melissa officinalis)*

Parsley *(Petroselinum crispum)*

Passion flower *(Passiflora incarnata)*

Peppermint *(Mentha piperita)*

Red Clover *(Trifolium pratense)*

Rosemary *(Salvia rosmarinus)*

Tulsi or holy basil *(Ocimum sanctum)*

## Macerates

Cleavers (Galium aparine) leaves and stems can be prepared as a macerate.

Marshmallow Root (Althaea officinalis) should be prepared as a macerate.

## Want to sweeten your tea?

Herbalist Julie James has a free ebook titled 'Herbal Honeys.'Download your copy here:
www.greenwisdomherbalstudies.com/ebook

Teas That I Would Like to Try

_____

_____


For more information, read "Medicinal Uses for Herbal Teas: Evidence, Dosing, and Preparation Methods" from the University of Wisconsin Integrative Health program:
www.fammed.wisc.edu/files/webfm-uploads/documents/outreach/im/ss_herbal_teas.pdf

# CHAPTER 6:

# ORGANIZE YOUR KITCHEN

## Why Focus on The Kitchen?

First things first. If we are going to focus on delicious and nutritious food during our recovery, we have to have an organized place to create our meals. This can become complicated if other family members aren't interested in changing their eating habits. There is not a one-size-fits-all solution. Let's explore a few questions to put together a list of what will work best for you.

Figure out if your home environment is making healthier eating habits more difficult by reading the article "3 Diet Experiments That Can Change Your Eating Habits—And Transform Your Body (Even If They Seem Way Too Easy To Work)," available at www.precisionnutrition.com/3-diet-experiments-to-change-eating-habits.

## What has worked before?

What techniques have worked for you before to promote eating nutritious food? Keeping a fruit bowl on the counter? Making a shopping list ahead of time?

_____

_____

## Making changes to your kitchen: Problems and Solutions

Ask your surgeon for details on any limitations you might have in the weeks after surgery.

**Problem:**

Some patients with breast augmentation are discouraged from heavy lifting, which means they cannot use large pots or cast iron for cooking. Some surgeons also discourage clients from lifting their arms above shoulder height.

**Solutions:**

- Use smaller pots and ask for help if heavy items need to be lifted
- Cook and freeze individual food portions before surgery
- Move needed items from top of refrigerator to lower space in the kitchen
- Move needed items from higher shelves to lower shelves

**Problem:** Patients often cannot stand straight after their tummy tuck and won't be able to reach higher shelves comfortably.

## Solutions:

- Relocate commonly used items on lower shelves
- Use a grabbing tool on a pole to help reach things
- Use a walker, stool or chair to rest on while cooking
- Involve other family members in cooking

What are some precautions your surgeon has advised?

_____

_____

Can you clear out a lower shelf in the pantry and a section of the refrigerator for your meals and snacks? Where will your post-surgery food be located in your kitchen?

_____

_____

**"**_Copper: Have you tried drinking out of a copper cup? In the article "Metallic Copper as an Antimicrobial Surface," microbiologist Gregor Grass et al. (2011) state that "copper surfaces, with their self-sanitizing properties, could be envisioned as making an important contribution to infection control. Thus, the use of antimicrobial metallic copper surfaces is likely to provide protection from infectious microbes by reducing surface contamination, as was recently shown in successful hospital trials._**"**

## Organizing snacks

**Problem:**

Recovery from surgery can be so tiring that many people will feel discouraged from eating healthy foods if they are too much hassle to prepare.

**Solutions:**

- Different-sized baskets may help keep snacks and side dishes organized.

- An over-the-door shoe organizer placed in your pantry can hold snacks.

- A tray with different sections may help to organize tea bags and can be placed next to your tea kettle and mugs.

What can you try to organize your snacks?

_____

_____

## Where to store spices?

Fresh herbs and spices can be grown in a garden on a balcony or windowsill and picked right before you need them. Dried herbs and spices can be stored on a shelf away from heat and light sources or in dark bottles on your counter.

Where will you keep your dried herbs and spices?

_____

_____

What are some other tips you have discovered that make your kitchen more organized?

_____

_____

## Meal planning

Have you tried planning out meals for the week and preparing a shopping list before you go to the grocery store or placing an online order for groceries?

What problems have you encountered and how can you solve them?

_____

_____

_____

_____

Can you gather all the tools you will need for meal prep so they are within reach when you are cooking? Where will you store your meal prep tools?

_____

_____

What are some other tips you have discovered that make meal planning easier?

_____

_____

## How to measure portions

Here are the official MyPlate recommendations for portion size and how to measure portions with your own hands:

- 1 serving of protein dense food is the size of your palm (or a deck of cards)
- 1 serving vegetables is the size of your fist or a baseball
- 1 serving of carbohydrates can fit into a cupped hand or a tennis ball or a CD case
- 1 serving fatty foods (nuts or oils) is the size of your thumb
- For more information on MyPlate, see choosemyplate. gov.

# CHAPTER 7:

# OUR GRANDMOTHER'S KITCHEN—RECOVERY RECIPES FROM SEVERAL CULTURES

Remember my friend who was in the ICU? He helped himself heal physically and emotionally by cooking and eating traditional "good for health" healing recipes from his culture.

What foods would older relatives make for you when you were sick?

When I asked friends for their family recipes, I found that there were two different types-simple, easily digestible foods for soothing an upset stomach and spicy, flavorful, and nutritious foods for nourishing the body. I've included both kinds here.

Because Southern Californians come from all over the world, these recipes are from several different cultures. The names and ingredients may be different from their more traditional versions.

Let's recap the names of some of the foods and spices we learned about earlier in the book:

Basil, black pepper, calendula, cantaloupe, chili peppers, chamomile, cinnamon, citrus fruits, cloves, cumin, dandelion, garlic, ginger, gotu kola, echinacea, kiwi fruit, lavender, lemon balm, marjoram, onions, parsley, papaya, paprika, passion flower, peppermint, pineapple, red clover, rosemary, tarragon, tulsi or holy basil and turmeric.

I'll be including a few of these in the following recipes. Hopefully you will be inspired to incorporate them into your own family recipes!

## Smoothies

**Blueberry smoothie**

**Cucumber pineapple ginger smoothie**

**Grapefruit papaya avocado smoothie**

**Nopal papaya pineapple smoothie**

**Papaya pineapple kiwi smoothie**

## Broths and Soups

**Pure chicken broth**

**Fish bone broth**

**Broccoli and cauliflower soup**

**Chicken noodle soup**

**Matzo ball soup**

**Congee**

**Cabbage and tomato soup**

Sopa de Aguada

# Brunch and Light Meals

**Broccoli cheddar quiche muffin**

**Dal and moong beans**

**Lentil coconut dal**

**Pumpkin pie overnight oats with pecans and cacao nibs**

**Kichadi**

**Dinner**

**Zucchini spaghetti with arugula pesto**

**Seafood spaghetti**

**Black bean burger**

**Lavender risotto**

**Spinach and chard ravioli**

**Salads and Side Dishes**

**Vegetable salad**

**Tasty spinach balls**

**Leafy greens salad**

**Fruit and vegetable**

**Salad**

**Guacamole with garlic and jalapenos**

**Mixed bean salad**

**Yogurt with avocado and za'atar**

## SMOOTHIES

Making a smoothie in the blender may be an easy way to feed yourself a snack when you might feel too tired or tender in the tummy to eat a full meal. Ingredients can be prepared in advance and refrigerated in a container until you want to blend. You can easily add protein powder to these recipes if you want to increase protein intake.

The trick with some of these smoothies is to not blend them completely. Leave some chunks!

# Blueberry Smoothie

**2 servings**

**Preparation time: 5 minutes**

**Cooking time: none**

## Ingredients

- 2 cups frozen blueberries
- 1 ½ frozen banana
- ½ cup almond milk (you can add more to bring smoothie to your favorite consistency)
- 1 tablespoon chia seeds

## Instructions

Add all ingredients in a high-speed blender and blend until smooth and creamy. Enjoy.

### *Additional tips*

- If you would like a thicker smoothie add more frozen bananas.

# Cucumber Pineapple Smoothie

**2 servings**

**Preparation time: 5 minutes**

**Cooking time: none**

## Ingredients

- 1 cup water (you can add more to bring smoothie to your favorite consistency)
- 1 cup pineapple, diced
- 1 medium cucumber, diced
- ½ banana
- ¼ cup fresh parsley
- 1 tablespoon ginger, peeled
- Juice of ½ lemon
- 1 teaspoon vanilla extract
- 1 teaspoon chia seeds
- Protein powder (optional)

## Instructions

Combine all ingredients in a high-speed blender and blend until smooth and creamy. Serve immediately and enjoy!

### Additional tips

- You can freeze the other half of the banana and add it to your smoothie tomorrow, which will help make it colder.

- When choosing a protein powder there are a few options; usually they are either whey, soy, or pea protein. Many are flavored chocolate, vanilla, or strawberry with artificial sweeteners. For this recipe, I suggest a plain, unflavored, unsweetened protein powder.

  You may need to add water to get it to your desired consistency.

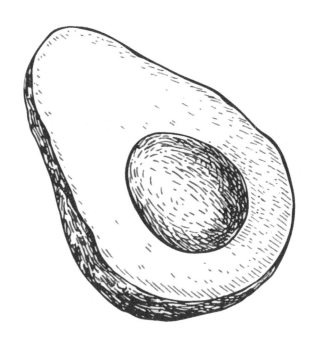

# Grapefruit, Papaya and Avocado Smoothie

**2 servings**

**Preparation time: 10 minutes**

**Cooking time: none**

## Ingredients

- 1 cup water (you can add more to bring smoothie to your favorite consistency)
- ½ cup baby spinach
- ½ cup papaya, peeled and seeded
- ½ medium avocado
- Juice of ½ lemon
- 1 grapefruit, peeled
- 1 banana, fresh or frozen
- 1 tablespoon whole flaxseeds

## Instructions

Add all ingredients to your blender and blend until smooth and creamy. Serve immediately and enjoy.

### Additional tips

- Make sure that you are not taking any medications that interact with grapefruit and it's enzymes.
- When storing the remaining avocado, cover it with lemon or lime juice and seal it with a plastic wrap. The next day, you may need to remove the brown layer on top, but it will be bright green underneath.
- Make sure to wash all your fruits including papaya and avocado. Even though you don't eat the skin, you could transfer bacteria from the skin into the flesh when you cut it.

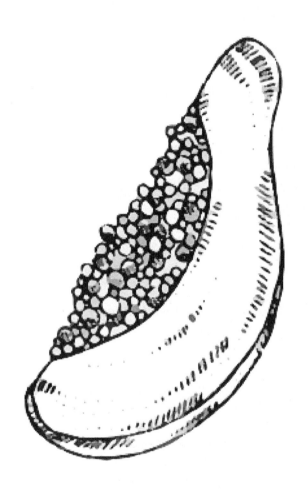

# Nopal Papaya and Pineapple Smoothie

**2 servings**

**Preparation time: 5 minutes**

**Cooking time: none**

## Ingredients

- 1 cup water (you can add more to bring smoothie to your favorite consistency)
- ¾ cup nopal, fresh, cleaned, with the spines removed; or canned
- 1 papaya, peeled, deseeded
- 1 cup pineapple, fresh or frozen
- Juice of 1 lime
- 1 tablespoon chia seeds

## Instructions

Combine all ingredients in a high-speed blender and blend until chunky, about 20 seconds. Serve immediately and enjoy.

## Additional tips

- Nopales are cactus pads. If you are buying the pad with the spines still on, you will have to carefully remove the spines. You can do this by holding the pad with some tongs and use a knife to scrape off the spines. You can cut off the edge of the pad or use a vegetable peeler.

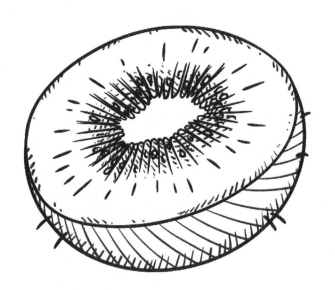

# Papaya, Pineapple, and Kiwi Smoothie

**2 servings**

**Preparation time: 5 minutes**

**Cooking time: none**

### Ingredients

- 1 cup water (you can add more to bring smoothie to your favorite consistency)
- 1 cup papaya, chopped
- 1 cup pineapple, chopped
- 2 kiwis, peeled, cut in half
- ¼ cup mint leaves
- 1 tablespoon whole flaxseeds

### Instructions

Add all ingredients to a high-speed blender and blend until chunky, about 20 seconds Serve immediately and enjoy.

## *Your Own Favorite Other smoothie recipes to try:*

### Recipe

**Directions**

_____
_____
_____
_____
_____
_____
_____
_____
_____
_____
_____

**Ingredients**

_____
_____
_____
_____
_____
_____
_____

### Recipe

**Directions**

_____
_____
_____
_____
_____
_____
_____
_____
_____
_____
_____

**Ingredients**

_____
_____
_____
_____
_____
_____
_____

## *Other smoothie combinations to try:*

Combine water with chunks of grapefruit, papaya and 1 tsp flaxseed.

Blend together water, chunks of papaya, nopales and chia or flaxseed.

Combine water with cucumber slices, lime juice and 1 tbsp chia seeds.

Blend together water or dandelion tea with 3 slices papaya, 2 slices pineapple, 1 tbsp flaxseed.

# BROTHS AND SOUPS

## Pure Chicken Broth

**4 servings**

**Preparation time: 20 minutes**

**Cooking time: 75 minutes**

### Ingredients

- 1 tablespoon vegetable oil (I recommend either extra-virgin olive oil or high-oleic sunflower or safflower oil)
- 1 yellow onion, cut into medium dice
- 2 carrots, peeled and diced
- 2 celery stalks, diced
- 1 garlic clove, minced
- 1 ½ lbs. chicken thighs, trimmed of excess fat, cut into pieces
- 1 ½ lbs. chicken legs, bone-in, trimmed of excess fat, cut into pieces
- 8 cups water
- 2 bay leaves
- Other herbs, optional—rosemary, thyme, savory, and sage all go well with chicken.

### Instructions

In a large, heavy-bottomed pot, heat the oil over medium-high heat. Add onion, carrots, celery, and garlic. Cook and stir for approximately 4 to 5 minutes. Add chicken and sauté for 5 minutes until the chicken is no longer pink. Cover with a lid and reduce the heat to low. Continue cooking for about 10 to 15 minutes until the chicken releases its juices, stirring occasionally. After 20 minutes, turn the heat to high and add the water and bay leaves. When the water begins to boil, reduce the heat to low, cover with a lid, and let the chicken broth simmer for 30 more minutes to develop its flavors. When done, strain the soup through a sieve or strainer to remove the solids. Voila, your chicken broth is ready to use. Enjoy! You can use this broth on its own as a light, nourishing light meal or for the chicken soup recipe below.

## Additional tips

- You can serve the broth with vegetables and chicken meat without straining it, as desired.
- Season with a few drops of extra virgin olive oil and fresh black pepper.

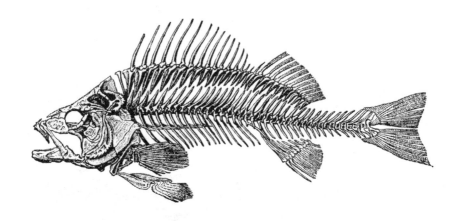

# Fish Bone Broth

**4–6 servings**

**Preparation time: 10 minutes**

**Cooking time: 2 hours and 40 minutes**

## Ingredients

- 2 lbs. fish bones (heads and carcasses from non-oily fish)
- 1 tablespoon butter or ghee
- 1 cup peeled and cubed celery root
- 2 carrots, peeled
- 1 medium yellow onion, peeled, quartered
- 1 leek, halved and cleaned well
- 3 cloves garlic
- 1 tablespoon black peppercorns
- 1 bay leaf
- 1 tablespoon apple cider vinegar
- ½ cup chopped parsley
- Water – enough to cover the fish bones

## Instructions

Use a large stockpot and add all ingredients except water. Carefully pour the water into the stockpot until all the bones and fish carcasses are just covered. Heat over medium heat and bring to a boil. Lower the heat and let it simmer for 2 hours, stirring every 15 minutes. Turn off the heat and let the broth sit for 30 minutes. Pour through a sieve to separate the broth from the solid ingredients. Pour the broth into a big glass jar with a lid and store in the fridge.

Enjoy!

# Broccoli and Cauliflower Soup

**4 servings**

**Preparation time: 10 minutes**

**Cooking time: 5 to 7 minutes**

## Ingredients

- ½ cup raw unsalted almonds
- 1 garlic clove, minced
- 1 ½ cup broccoli florets, chopped
- 1 ½ cup cauliflower florets, chopped
- 1 1/3 cup vegetable broth
  ¼ teaspoon ginger, grated
  ¼ teaspoon curry powder
- ¼ teaspoon garlic powder
- Extra virgin olive oil
- Black pepper, to taste

## Instructions

Add almonds, garlic, broccoli and cauliflower in a food processor and process until you have small chunks.

Add in vegetable broth, spices, and process again until smooth and creamy.

Pour the mixture in a saucepan and cook over medium heat for 5 to 7 minutes.

Season with extra virgin olive oil and pepper.

Serve and enjoy.

### Additional info

- Add more broth if needed to reach the desired consistency.
- You can garnish the soup with chopped chives, croutons, or seeds.

# Chicken Noodle Soup

**2–4 servings**

**Preparation time: 10 minutes**

**Cooking time: 1 hour and 30 minutes**

## Ingredients

- ½ pound chicken legs, bone-in
- ¼ teaspoon black pepper
- 1 tablespoon extra-virgin olive oil
- ½ large yellow onion, chopped
- 1 garlic clove, minced
- 4 cups chicken broth (use Pure Chicken Broth recipe, or a commercially available organic chicken broth)
- 1 carrot, chopped
- 1 stalk celery, chopped
- 1 bay leaf
- ½ tsp fresh thyme, or ¼ tsp dried
- 2/3 cup uncooked egg noodles
- 2/3 tsp lemon juice
- 1 tsp chopped fresh parsley

## Instructions

Pat the chicken legs dry using paper towels and rub with pepper. Set aside.

In a large stockpot, heat the oil over medium-high heat and add the chicken in batches, skin side down. Cook for 3-5 minutes until golden brown, then turn over and let cook for another 3-5 minutes. Remove the chicken and transfer to a plate. Set aside.

Add the onion to the stockpot and cook for 5 minutes over medium-high heat while stirring.

Add the garlic and cook for another minute. Then add the chicken broth and bring to a boil. Add the chicken legs back into the stockpot, then add carrots, celery, bay leaves, and thyme. Reduce heat to a simmer, cover with a lid and cook for 25–30 minutes until the chicken is tender.

Remove the lid and transfer the chicken to a plate. Set aside.

Add the noodles to the stockpot, cover with the lid again and let it simmer for about 20 minutes, until the noodles are al dente (or however you like your noodles).

In the meantime, remove the chicken meat from the bones and use a fork to shred the meat into small pieces.

Remove the soup from the heat and add the shredded meat to the stockpot. Stir in the lemon juice and parsley. Taste and add more pepper if needed.

Discard the bay leaf and divide the soup between serving dishes. Enjoy!

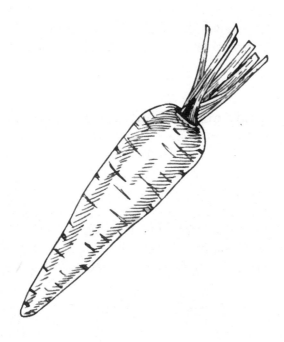

# Matzo Ball Soup

**4 servings**

**Preparation time: 5 minutes**

**Cooking time: 1 hour and 30 minutes**

## Ingredients

- 2 tablespoons vegetable oil
- 2 eggs, lightly beaten
- 1 teaspoon freshly chopped flat-leaf parsley
- A pinch of white pepper
- ½ cup matzo meal
- 1 tablespoon water
- 6 cups chicken broth (use pure chicken broth above or a commercially available organic chicken broth)
- 1 medium carrot, peeled, cut into thin slices or strips

## Instructions

Add oil and eggs in a medium bowl, and stir to combine. Add parsley, pepper, matzo meal, and water.

Stir until all ingredients are well combined, forming a soft dough. Cover and place it in the fridge for at least 30 minutes.

Add the chicken broth and carrots to a large pot and bring to a boil, then reduce the heat to a simmer.

Take the dough out of the fridge. Dip your hands in cold water and form the matzo dough into 6 balls.

Drop the matzo balls into the simmering broth and cook, covered, for 30 minutes.

Divide between soup bowls and enjoy.

# Congee

**4 servings**

**Preparation time: 5 minutes**

**Cooking time: 1 hour**

## Ingredients

- 9 cups bone broth
- 2 tablespoons finely chopped ginger
- 2 cups cremini mushrooms, wiped with a damp towel
- ¾ cup long-grain rice
- 2 tablespoons ghee
- Optional toppings (see note below)

## Instructions

Take a large pot and add bone broth of your choice, ginger and mushrooms. Turn the heat to high and bring it to a quick boil. Reduce the heat to medium-low and let it simmer, uncovered, for 40 minutes until the broth is thickened.
Add the rice and continue cooking until the rice is cooked.
Stir the ghee into the congee and add any of the optional toppings you like. Divide between bowls and enjoy!

### Additional tips

*Optional Toppings:*
Chopped ginger, fresh scallions, gluten-free tamari, coconut aminos, or sesame oil.

*Optional Herbs:*
Parsley, cilantro, mint, or basil.

# Cabbage and Tomato Soup

**3–4 servings**

**Preparation Time: 10 minutes**

**Cooking time: 35 minutes**

## Ingredients

- 6 cups organic beef broth
- ½ green cabbage, chopped
- ½ stalk celery, chopped
- 1 clove garlic, minced
- ½ cup chopped yellow onion
- ½ teaspoon black pepper
- 14 oz. canned tomatoes, diced (Italian style)

## Instructions

In a large stockpot, add organic beef broth, cabbage, celery, garlic, and onion.

Turn heat to high and bring to a quick boil. Add pepper and tomatoes. Stir and reduce heat to a simmer.

Cook covered for 30 minutes or until the cabbage is cooked through and the flavors have developed.

Remove from the heat and divide between soup bowls.

Enjoy!

# Sopa Aguada

**4 servings**

**Preparation time: 10 minutes**

**Cooking time: 35 minutes**

## Ingredients

- ¼ yellow onion
- ½ garlic clove
- 2 ripe tomatoes, peeled and chopped
- 2 tablespoon vegetable oil
- 7 oz. small dry pasta (dots, alphabet…)
- 6 cups organic chicken broth (use pure chicken broth above, or a commercially available organic chicken broth)
- 3 limes, cut into wedges
- 2 stalks parsley, fresh, chopped, for decoration

## Instructions

Place the onion, garlic and tomatoes into a high-speed blender and blend until well combined.

Heat the oil in a medium-sized saucepan and add the dry pasta into the hot oil.

Fry the pasta while stirring continuously until most of it has turned light brown in color. Be careful not to burn your pasta.

Next, add the blended tomato mixture and the chicken broth to the saucepan, stir well, bring to a boil and simmer for 15 or 20 minutes. Divide into serving dishes, sprinkle with parsley, and serve with lime wedges.

# Your Own Favorite Recipes

## Recipe

### Directions

_____
_____
_____
_____
_____
_____
_____
_____
_____
_____

### Ingredients

_____
_____
_____
_____
_____
_____
_____
_____

## Recipe

### Directions

_____
_____
_____
_____
_____
_____
_____
_____
_____
_____

### Ingredients

_____
_____
_____
_____
_____
_____
_____
_____

# BRUNCH

## Asparagus Cheddar Quiche Muffins

**Servings: 6 muffins**

**Preparation time: 10 minutes**

**Cooking time: 40 minutes**

### Ingredients

- 1 cup cooked quinoa
- 6 stalks asparagus, cut in one-inch pieces, tips reserved for decoration
- ½ teaspoon garlic powder
- 2 tablespoons chopped chives
- ½ cup reduced fat shredded cheddar cheese
- ½ teaspoon paprika powder
- ½ teaspoon cayenne pepper
- 1 egg
- 1 egg white

### Instructions

Preheat the oven to 350°F and grease a muffin pan with oil.

Cook the quinoa according to package instructions. When the quinoa is done, set it aside.

Add the cut-up asparagus stalks (minus the tips) to a medium-size bowl.

Mix in cooked quinoa, garlic, chives, cheddar cheese, paprika, cayenne pepper, and egg.

Mix until well combined, then spoon the mixture evenly into the muffin pan. Arrange the asparagus tips on top of each quiche muffin and place the pan in the oven. Bake for 20 minutes or until cooked and lightly brown.

Remove muffin tin from the oven.

Allow the muffins to cool and enjoy!

Cheese is high in salt, so only try this recipe if your swelling is under control.

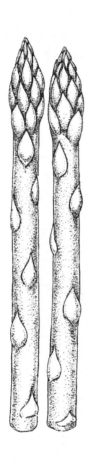
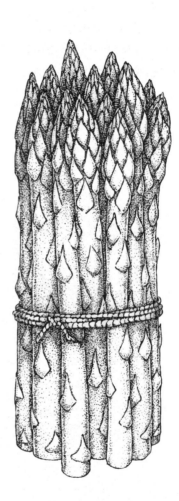

## Dal and Moong Beans

Lentils are a high-protein pulse crop. They provide significant amounts of essential nutrients for healthy living. Cook lentils (after soaking them) in a rice cooker with diced vegetables and spices of your choice and add 3 cups of water for every cup of lentils. Dal can be made bland or with added spices. Or try the next recipe for a more complex dish.

Kathleen Helen Lisson, CLT

# Lentil Coconut Dal

**2 servings**

**Preparation time: 15 minutes**

**Cooking time: 40 minutes**

## Ingredients

- 2 tablespoons water
- ½ cup finely chopped red onion
- 1 ½ cloves garlic, minced
- 1 ½ teaspoon minced or grated fresh ginger
- 2 ¼ teaspoons curry powder
- ¾ teaspoon cumin
- 1/8 teaspoon red pepper flakes
- 1 ¼ cups organic vegetable broth
- ½ cup canned organic coconut milk
- ¾ cup dry red lentils, rinsed and drained
- ¼ cup chopped fresh cilantro
- 2 teaspoon lime juice

## Instructions

Heat the water in a large pot over medium heat. Add the onion, garlic, and ginger to the pot and cook until the water evaporates, about 5 to 7 minutes.

Stir in the curry powder, cumin, and red pepper flakes and cook for another minute until very fragrant.

Add the vegetable broth and coconut milk to the pot, add the lentils, and stir well to combine. Bring the lentils to a gentle boil then reduce heat to medium-low. Let it simmer for 25 to 30 minutes or until the lentils are tender.

Remove from the heat. Stir in the cilantro and lime juice.

Pour into bowls and enjoy!

# Pumpkin Pie Overnight Oats with Pecans and Cacao Nibs

**2-3 servings**

**Preparation Time: 5 minutes**

**Cooking time: 8 hours**

## Ingredients

- 1 cup pureed pumpkin
- 1 cup organic slow cook oatmeal, dry
- 1 tablespoon chia seeds
- 1 ½ teaspoon pumpkin pie spice
- 2 tablespoons maple syrup
- 1 cup unsweetened almond milk
- ¼ cup chopped pecans
- 1 tablespoon cacao nibs

## Instructions

In a medium bowl, combine the pumpkin puree, oats, chia seeds, pumpkin pie spice, maple syrup, and almond milk. Stir well to combine, cover, and store in your fridge overnight or until set.

Divide into serving dishes, top with pecans and cacao nibs.

Enjoy.

# Kichadi / Kichdi

**3 servings**

**Preparation time: 5 minutes**

**Cooking time: 30 minutes**

## Ingredients

- 1 cup basmati rice
- 2 cups water
- ½ cup mung/moong beans, dal, or other lentil
- 2 tablespoon ghee
- 2 cups diced vegetables (e.g., onions and tomatoes)
- 1 tablespoon Banyan Botanicals kitchari spice mix or a similar brand in your local Indian market

## Instructions

Add rice, water, and lentils to a rice cooker or pot and cook. While the rice mixture is cooking, sauté vegetables in oil until onions are golden in color.

Stir the spice mix and cooked vegetables into the rice mixture.

Divide between bowls and enjoy!

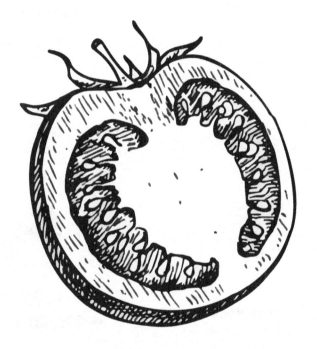

# Your Own Favorite Recipes

## Recipe

### Directions

### Ingredients

## Recipe

### Directions

### Ingredients

# DINNER

## Zucchini Spaghetti with Arugula Pesto

**4 servings**

**Preparationtime: 15 minutes**

**Cooking time: none**

### Ingredients

- 4 cups arugula
- ½ cup almonds
- 1 cup Parmigiano Reggiano cheese, grated
- 1 garlic clove
- Black pepper (optional)
- 2/3 cup extra virgin olive oil
- 4 small zucchini
- Juice of ¼ lemon

### Instructions

Add arugula, almonds, cheese and garlic clove (and pepper if using) to a food processor. Process while gradually adding extra virgin olive oil. Continue processing until you obtain a creamy pesto sauce. Peel zucchini with a noodle peeler and season with a few drops of lemon juice.
Combine zucchini noodles with Arugula pesto.
Serve immediately and enjoy.

### *Additional tips*

- Cheese is high in salt, so only try this recipe if your swelling is under control.
- You can prepare many delicious pesto sauces for zucchini noodles.
- Garnish the dish with paprika powder, basil leaves or chopped chives.
- You can add a crunchy texture to the dish with a tablespoon of chopped toasted nuts.

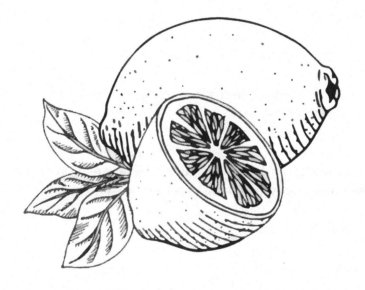

# Seafood Spaghetti

**4 servings**

**Preparation time: 20 minutes**

**Cooking time: 17–20 minutes**

## Ingredients

- 1.5 lb. mussels
- 1.5 lb. clams
- 10 oz. spaghetti
- 4 large shrimps (or 8 small shrimps)
- 5 tbsp Extra virgin olive oil (divided)
- 2 garlic cloves, minced
- 1 large squid, cleaned and cut into small strips
- 1 tablespoon parsley, chopped
- ½ teaspoon tomato paste
- 1 cup plum cherry tomatoes, cut into quarters
- 2 ½ tablespoons green olives, sliced (olives are high in salt)
- 1 teaspoon capers (optional, as capers are high in salt)
- A pinch of chili powder
- Black pepper, to taste

## Instructions

Clean the mussels by pinching off the beards. Rinse mussels and clams under cold running water and place them in a mixing bowl with salted water (seawater if possible) and refrigerate for at least 2 hours. Rinse them again under cold running water and place them in a colander. Remove all the broken clams and mussels. Bring a large pot with water to a boil and cook spaghetti according to package instructions. In a large skillet, heat 2 tablespoons of extra virgin olive oil over medium heat. Add clams and mussels, cover the skillet with a lid, and cook for 2–3 minutes until they open up. Do not use any that don't open. Remove the skillet from heat and place the clams and mussels in a heatproof bowl. Let cool and cut the meat out of the shells with a knife. Heat 3 tablespoons of extra virgin olive oil in a large skillet over medium heat. Add garlic and cook for 20 seconds. Add squid strips and chopped parsley, and cook for 3 minutes. Stir occasionally. Add tomato paste, plum cherry tomatoes and olives, and cook for an additional 7 minutes, stirring frequently. Add in shrimp, clams, and mussels. Season with pepper, chili powder and stir well. Cook for an additional 3 minutes. Drain spaghetti, add to the skillet, and stir well to combine. Remove from the heat and serve.

### Additional tips

- Capers and olives are high in salt, so only try this recipe if your swelling is under control.
- Drain the pasta when 'al dente'—cooked, but still firm to the bite
- Garnish the dish with chopped chives, basil leaves or cilantro.

# Black Bean Burger

**4 servings**

**Preparation time: 10 minutes**

**Cooking time: 5 minutes**

## Ingredients

- 1 can black beans
- 1 small red bell pepper
- 1 small green bell pepper
- 1 red onion
- 1 garlic clove
- 3 tablespoons breadcrumbs
- ½ teaspoon onion powder
- 1/3 teaspoon garlic powder
- ½ teaspoon chili powder
- 1 1/3 tablespoon cornstarch
- 1 tablespoon cold water
- Black pepper, to taste
- ½ tablespoon freshly chopped parsley
- Extra-virgin olive oil

## Instructions

Drain and rinse black beans and place them in a food processor with bell peppers, onion, and garlic clove. Process the ingredients into small chunks.

Transfer the mixture to a bowl; add breadcrumbs, spices, cornstarch, water, black pepper, and parsley.

Mix well and form 4 patties with wet hands.

Heat 1 tablespoon of extra virgin olive oil in a non-stick pan over medium heat. Cook patties for about 2 minutes per side.

## Additional tips

- Serve bean burgers with steamed vegetables, fresh salad, or grilled vegetables like zucchini or eggplant.
- Use extra virgin olive oil, freshly chopped herbs, lemon juice and spices to season your meal.

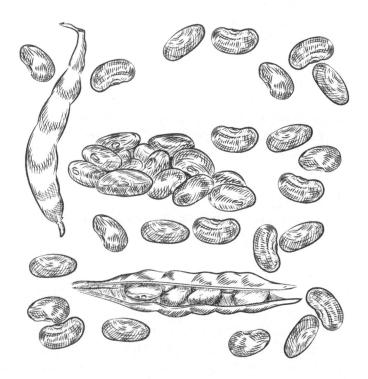

# Lavender Risotto

**4 servings**

**Preparation time: 10 minutes**

**Cooking time: 35-40 minutes**

## Ingredients

- Approx. 4 ¼ cups water
- 2 onions, peeled (divided)
- 1 large carrot, peeled
- 1 celery rib
- 4 stems of lavender
- 2 tablespoons butter
- 1 cup short-grain rice (see additional tips below)
- ¾ cup grated Parmigiano Reggiano cheese (this is high in salt)
- Black pepper, to taste

## Instructions

Pour water in a pot and place it over medium heat. Add in onion, carrot, celery, and lavender. Cook until it begins to boil, reduce the heat, cover, and continue cooking for an additional 15 to 20 minutes, then strain and return to the pot to keep warm.

Chop 1 onion. Melt the butter in a skillet and add chopped onion. Cook until translucent, then add the rice. Toast the rice for a minute. Add a ladle of strained broth and stir to incorporate the broth. Proceed by adding a ladle of lavender broth at a time until the rice is cooked. Remove from the heat, add grated cheese, and stir well with a wooden spoon.

Season with pepper.

Serve immediately.

## *Additional tips*

- When preparing risotto use only short grain rice like Vialone Nano, Carnaroli, or Arborio.
- Cook the rice until "al dente," which means cooked, but still firm to the bite.
- Garnish with lavender flowers, freshly chopped chives, or nuts.
- Cheese is high in salt, so only try this recipe if your swelling is under control.

# Kale Ravioli

**Approximately 25 ravioli**

**Preparation time: 40 minutes**

**Cooking time: 10–15 minutes**

## Ingredients

- Pasta dough
- 2 cups flour
- 2 eggs + 1 egg yolk
- *Filling*
- 8 large kale leaves, washed and cut into small strips
- 2/3 cup ricotta cheese
- 2 tablespoons grated Parmigiano cheese

## Instructions

In a large bowl mix flour and eggs. Knead well to obtain a homogeneous and smooth dough. Wrap the dough with plastic wrap and set aside. In a small pan, bring water to a boil. Add kale and boil it for a couple of minutes.

Drain kale strips and squeeze them to remove excess water. Mince them with a sharp chef knife. Place them in a mixing bowl.

Add ricotta cheese and grated Parmigiano cheese and mix well to combine.

Unwrap the dough and divide it into two equal portions. Roll each portion into thin rectangular sheets.

Distribute a spoonful of kale filling on one sheet, at a distance of about 1.5 inches one from the other.

Cover the first filled sheet with the second sheet and gently press the upper sheet around the filling with your fingers. Cut ravioli with a notched cutter wheel or sharp knife.

Cook ravioli for 4 to 5 minutes in boiling water.

## *Additional tips*

- Cheese is high in salt, so only try this recipe if your swelling is under control.
- Serve ravioli with meat, fish, or vegetable broth. You can also prepare simple sauces for ravioli like melted butter with sage or tomato sauce.

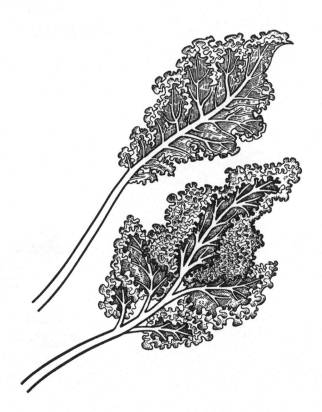

# Your Own Favorite Recipes

## Recipe

### Directions

_____
_____
_____
_____
_____
_____
_____
_____
_____
_____
_____

### Ingredients

_____
_____
_____
_____
_____
_____
_____
_____

## Recipe

### Directions

_____
_____
_____
_____
_____
_____
_____
_____
_____
_____
_____

### Ingredients

_____
_____
_____
_____
_____
_____
_____
_____

# SALADS AND SIDE DISHES

## Vegetable Salad

**4 servings**

**Preparation time: 15 minutes**

**Cooking time: none**

### Ingredients

- ½ cup lamb's lettuce (also known as mache)
- ½ cup baby spinach leaves
- ½ cup baby chard leaves
- 1 shallot, cut into thin slices
- 1 cup fat-free feta cheese, crumbled
- 15 black olives, pitted and sliced (olives are high in salt)
- 2/3 cup red cabbage, shredded
- ½ red bell pepper, seeded and diced
- ½ green bell pepper, seeded and diced
- ½ yellow bell pepper, seeded and diced
- 4 dry plums (prunes), pitted and diced
- 1 pear, cored and sliced (optional)

*Dressing*

- Extra virgin olive oil, to taste
- 1 tablespoon chives, chopped
- Balsamic vinegar (optional)

### Instructions

In a large serving bowl, combine all salad ingredients.
Season with extra virgin olive oil, chives, and balsamic vinegar.
Toss gently to coat and serve.
Enjoy.

## *Additional tips*

- Cheese and olives are high in salt, so only try this recipe if your swelling is under control.
- You can refrigerate this salad in an airtight container (without dressing) for up to 2 days.
- Add some crunchy texture with chopped nuts.
- You can replace sliced pear with apple.

# Tasty Spinach Balls

**Servings: 15 spinach balls**

**Preparation time: 15 minutes**

**Cooking time: 25 minutes**

## Ingredients

- 2 tablespoons extra-virgin olive oil
- 1 cup spinach leaves, cleaned and cut into strips
  1 cup ricotta cheese
- ½ cup grated Parmigiano Reggiano or Grana Padano cheese
- ½ cup breadcrumbs
- Black pepper, to taste

*Breading*

- 1 Egg
- Breadcrumbs to taste

## Instructions

Preheat oven to 390°F and line a baking sheet with parchment paper. Heat extra-virgin olive oil in a skillet over medium-high heat. Add spinach leaves and cook for 5 to 7 minutes until it has wilted down completely. Stir frequently.

Drain the spinach and remove excess water by pressing it with a spoon or use a potato ricer.

Place spinach on a cutting board and mince it.

In a medium bowl, combine minced spinach, ricotta, grated Parmigiano cheese, and breadcrumbs. Mix well to combine. Season with black pepper to taste and mix again.

Form 15 spinach balls and pass each one through beaten egg and breadcrumbs.

Arrange spinach balls on the baking sheet and bake for about 15 minutes.

Remove from the oven, let them cool, and serve.

## *Additional tips*

- Cheese is high in salt, so only try this recipe if your swelling is under control.
- Prepare a healthy dressing with Greek yogurt, minced garlic or garlic powder, cucumber and chopped chives.
- Serve with a fresh salad or as an appetizer.

# Leafy Greens Salad

**4 servings**

**Preparation time: 20 minutes**

**Cooking time: none**

## Ingredients

- 2 cups baby spinach leaves
- 1 cup baby chard leaves
- 1 cup baby kale leaves
- 1 cup lamb's lettuce (also known as mache)
- 1 avocado, pitted and sliced
- 1 apple, cored and sliced
- 2/3 cup cherry tomatoes, cut in quarters
- ½ cup almond slices

*Dressing*

- Extra virgin olive oil, to taste
- Lemon juice, to taste
- Black pepper, to taste

## Instructions

Combine salad ingredients in a large serving bowl.
Season with extra virgin olive oil, lemon juice, and pepper.
Toss to coat and serve.

## Additional tips

- You can replace almonds with other types of nuts like walnuts or pecans.
- Use healthy ingredients like extra virgin olive oil, apple cider vinegar, lemon or lime juice and zest, orange, etc. to season your salad.

# Fruit and Vegetable Salad

**4 servings**

**Preparation time: 15 minutes**

**Cooking time: none**

## Ingredients

- 1 pink grapefruit, peeled and cut into wedges
- 2 apples, cored and sliced
- 1 cup baby spinach
- 5 oz. mixed salad greens
- ½ cup fresh blueberries
- ½ cup walnuts, chopped

*Dressing*

- 3 tablespoons lemon juice
- 2 tablespoons extra virgin olive oil
- Maple syrup, to taste (optional)

## Instructions

In a large serving bowl combine all salad ingredients.
Season with lemon juice, extra virgin olive oil, and maple syrup.
Toss to coat and serve.
Enjoy it.

### Additional tips

Make sure that you are not taking any medications that interact with grapefruit and it's enzymes.
Fruit salads are always tastier if served cold, so you can cover the bowl and refrigerate the salad for an hour before serving (without dressing). Instead of maple syrup you can use balsamic vinegar glaze for more flavor.
Replace walnuts with almond slices or chopped pecans.
Grated Parmigiano cheese is a good match with veggie and fruit salads, but it is high in salt.

# Guacamole with Garlic and Jalapenos

**2 servings**

**Preparation time: 5 minutes**

**Cooking time: none**

## Ingredients

- 1 avocado
- ½ lime, juiced
- ½ cup cherry tomatoes, cut into quarters
- 1 garlic clove, minced
- A pinch of cumin
- A pinch of chili powder
- Black pepper, to taste
- ¼ medium jalapeno, sliced into small rings

## Instructions

Place avocado in a bowl and mash it well with a fork. Add lime juice, cherry tomatoes, garlic, cumin, and chili powder.
Season with pepper and stir well.
Transfer guacamole to a bowl, top with jalapeno rings and enjoy.

# Grilled Sardines

**4 servings**

**Preparation time: 10 minutes**

**Cooking time: 5 to 10 minutes**

## Ingredients

- 20 fresh sardines

*Mediterranean dressing*

- 2 tablespoons freshly chopped parsley
- 1 large garlic clove, minced
- 1 teaspoon lime zest
- A pinch of onion powder
- A pinch of chili powder (optional)
- 2 basil leaves, chopped
- 1 cup extra virgin olive oil
- Black pepper, to taste

## Instructions

Grill sardines until charred.
In a small jar combine all Mediterranean sauce ingredients and mix well to combine.
Place grilled sardines on a large serving plate.
Top with Mediterranean dressing.

### Additional tips

- Use Mediterranean dressing to season grilled fish like tuna or sea bass, or vegetable salads.
- Serve with simple and easy potato salad: Place potatoes in a pot and cover them with water. Cook until potatoes are fork-tender. Drain them and let cool. Peel the potatoes and cut them into thin rounds. Place potatoes in a serving bowl and season with extra virgin olive oil, chopped parsley and black pepper.

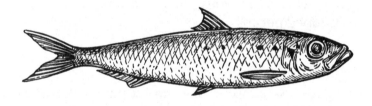

# Salmon Tartare with Avocado Cream

**4 servings**

**Preparation time: 30 minutes**

**Cooking time: none**

## Ingredients

- 14 oz. smoked salmon, cut into small strips
- A few drops of extra virgin olive oil
- 1 lime, juice and zest
- Black pepper, to taste
- 1 teaspoon chopped chives
  1 tablespoon rice vinegar
- 16 oz. avocado, peeled and cut in cubes
- ½ cup plum cherry tomatoes, cut in quarters
- ½ cup chopped pecans

## Instructions

Place salmon strips in a mixing bowl and season with a few drops of extra virgin olive oil, lime zest, black pepper, chives, and rice vinegar. Stir well, cover and place in the refrigerator for 20 to 30 minutes.

Place avocado cubes in a plate or a bowl, season with lime juice, and mash well with a fork.

Add plum cherry tomatoes, chopped pecans, and mix well to combine. Take small serving jars or cups and place a layer of avocado cream on the bottom. Top with marinated salmon.

### Additional info

- Garnish the dish with chopped fresh herbs, more chopped nuts, seeds, and season with a few drops of extra virgin olive oil.

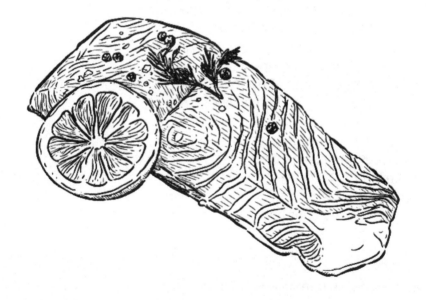

# Vegetable Quinoa Salad

**2 - 4 servings**

**Preparation time: 15 minutes**

**Cooking time: 18 minutes**

## Ingredients

- 1 ½ cup quinoa
- 1 red bell pepper, seeded and diced
- 1 green bell pepper, seeded and diced
- 15 plum cherry tomatoes, cut in quarters
- 15 black olives, diced (olives are high in salt)
- ½ cup crumbled feta cheese (optional, it is high in salt)
- 2/3 cup walnuts, chopped
- 1 tablespoon sliced almond
- 1 tablespoon chopped parsley
- 1 lime, zest and juice
- Zest of ½ orange
- 1 sweet onion, julienned
- Extra virgin olive oil
- Pepper, to taste
- 8 basil leaves, chopped

## Instructions

Prepare quinoa as indicated on the package.
In a large serving bowl mix cooked quinoa with the remaining ingredients.
Season with extra virgin olive oil and pepper, and toss gently.
Garnish with chopped basil leaves.

### Additional tips

- Cheese and olives are high in salt, so only try this recipe if your swelling is under control.

- You can replace walnuts with other types of nuts.
- To add more flavor, combine baby spinach leaves, Arugula or lamb's lettuce.
- Garnish with chopped chives or chopped parsley.

# Mixed Bean Salad

**2 servings**

**Preparation time: 10 minutes**

**Cooking time: none**

## Ingredients

- 1 cup cooked red kidney beans
- 1 cup cooked white navy beans
- 1 red onion, sliced
- 1 tomato, chopped
- ½ red bell pepper, diced
- ½ yellow bell pepper, diced
- ½ green bell pepper, diced
- ¼ cup chopped parsley
- ½ medium jalapeno, finely diced
- 2–3 tablespoons extra-virgin olive oil
- Juice of f ½ lemon
- Black pepper, to taste
- ¼ cup alfalfa or broccoli sprouts, for topping

## Instructions

In a large salad bowl, combine the red kidney beans, white navy beans, onion, tomato, bell peppers, parsley, and jalapeno. Toss to combine. In a small bowl, whisk together the olive oil and lemon juice, and pour over the mixed salad. Season with pepper and toss well until all ingredients are well coated.

Divide between salad bowls or plates and top with sprouts.

Enjoy.

# Yogurt with Avocado and Za'atar

Za'atar is a dried spice blend containing marjoram, oregano, sesame seeds, thyme and sumac. Use it with olive oil as a bread dip or to season vegetables or meat dishes.

**2 servings**

**Preparing time: 5 minutes**

**Cooking time: 10 minutes**

## Ingredients

- 1 cup cooked quinoa
- 1 ½ cups plain Greek yogurt (choose one with probiotics)
- ½ avocado, peeled, cut into slices
- 1 tablespoon extra-virgin olive oil
- 1 teaspoon za'atar spice
- ½ cup alfalfa sprouts
- ½ lemon (sliced)

## Instructions

Cook the quinoa according to package instructions.
While the quinoa is cooking, divide Greek yogurt between the plates.
Arrange sliced avocado and cooked quinoa on top of Greek yogurt.
Drizzle with olive oil and sprinkle with Za'atar.
Garnish with alfalfa sprouts and serve with lemon slices on the side.
Enjoy.

# Your Own Favorite Recipes

## Recipe

### Directions

_____
_____
_____
_____
_____
_____
_____
_____
_____

### Ingredients

_____
_____
_____
_____
_____
_____
_____
_____

## Recipe

### Directions

_____
_____
_____
_____
_____
_____
_____
_____
_____

### Ingredients

_____
_____
_____
_____
_____
_____
_____
_____

# Recipes from my own family and friends that I would like to try

## SHOPPING LIST

What will you need in the kitchen when you are meal prepping after surgery? Write down your preferences now so you can easily let family and friends know what to keep stocked after your surgery.

Favorite fruits:

_____

_____

_____

Favorite vegetables:

_____

_____

_____

Red and orange vegetables

_____

_____

_____

Dark green vegetables (leafy greens and others)

_____

_____

_____

Other favorite vegetables:

_____

_____

_____

Favorite legumes

_____

_____

_____

Favorite low-fat dairy foods

_____

_____

_____

# Favorite protein foods (meat, seafood, nuts, seeds)

_____

_____

_____

# Favorite cooking oils

_____

_____

_____

# Favorite spices

_____

_____

_____

# Favorite dips and sauces

_____

_____

_____

Favorite whole grain breads and crackers

_____

_____

_____

Favorite snacks

_____

_____

_____

Find guidelines for the Mediterranean-Style eating pattern at health.gov/our-work/food-nutrition/2015-2020-dietary-guidelines/guidelines/appendix-4/

# CHAPTER 8:

# FOOD FOR THOUGHT

If you enjoy journaling, here are some questions to write about.

What are your concerns about your wellness, eating habits, or fitness level?

What are you ready and willing to do to achieve your fitness and nutrition goals?

What have you tried in the past to improve your diet, nutrition, or fitness level? What has worked well for you? What hasn't worked so well? How would you like your eating habits to be different? Who does the grocery shopping in your home? Who does the cooking? Are you following a specific way of eating? How long have you been doing so? What are some foods you like? What are some foods you don't like?

Have you made changes recently to your self-care eating or fitness habits? Are there any additional changes you would like to make? What has held you back from making those changes? What situations interfere with your normal eating habits and get you off track? Rate your eating habits from 1-10

How active are you? How many hours a week are dedicated to physical activity? What types of physical activity, exercise, play or movement do you like? How would you like your fitness habits to be different? Rate your fitness habits from 1-10

Do family, friends and other people in your life support your eating and fitness behavior changes?

What is your stress level? How many hours do you sleep? How much water do you drink, in ounces, per day? What self-care activities help you lower stress? Have you tried anything in the past to improve your stress level? What has worked well for you? What hasn't worked so well? How would you like your self-care habits to be different? What self-care practices can you use in the week before surgery?

# CONCLUSION

You have just finished reading the cookbook I wish I had on hand when I was recovering from surgery. I am so thrilled to be able to share Registered Dietician Jean LaMantia's wisdom as well as a variety of academic journal articles. Please check with your plastic surgeon or physician before beginning any nutrition or exercise program. I have provided links to the academic journal articles discussed in the book so you can have it on hand when you plan your recovery with your plastic surgeon.

## Resources

Find links to the websites shared in the book and more at SouthernCaliforniaPlasticSurgeryCookbook.com

# REFERENCES

Altun, I., & Kurutaş, E. B. (2016). Vitamin B complex and vitamin B12 levels after peripheral nerve injury. *Neural regeneration research, 11*(5), 842–845. doi:10.4103/1673-5374.177150 Retrieved from: https://www.ncbi.nlm.nih.gov/pmc/articles/PMC4904479/

Becic, T., Studenik, C., & Hoffmann, G. (2018). Exercise Increases Adiponectin and Reduces Leptin Levels in Prediabetic and Diabetic Individuals: Systematic Review and Meta-Analysis of Randomized Controlled Trials. *Medical sciences (Basel, Switzerland), 6*(4), 97. https://doi.org/10.3390/medsci6040097. Retrieved from: https://www.ncbi.nlm.nih.gov/pmc/articles/PMC6318757/

Bhagat, S. Agarwal, M., & Roy, V. (2013). "Serratiopeptidase: A systematic review of the existing evidence". International journal of surgery (London, England). 11. 10.1016/j.ijsu.2013.01.010. Retrieved from: https://www.researchgate.net/publication/235400237_Serratiopeptidase_A_systematic_review_of_the_existing_evidence

Bohl, D., Shen, M., Kayupov, E., & Valle, C. (2015). Hypoalbuminemia Independently Predicts Surgical Site Infection, Pneumonia, Length of Stay, and Readmission After Total Joint Arthroplasty. The Journal of Arthroplasty. 31. 10.1016/j.arth.2015.08.028. Retrieved from: https://www.ncbi.nlm.nih.gov/pubmed/26427941

Brandt, S. L., & Serezani, C. H. (2017). Too much of a good thing: How modulating LTB4 actions restore host defense in homeostasis or disease. *Seminars in immunology, 33*, 37–43. https://doi.org/10.1016/j.smim.2017.08.006 Retrieved from: https://www.ncbi.nlm.nih.gov/pmc/articles/PMC5679129/

Briggs, P., Hawrylack, H. & Mooney, R. (2016). Inhaled peppermint oil for postop nausea in patients undergoing cardiac surgery. Nursing. 46. 61-67. 10.1097/01.NURSE.0000482882.38607.5c. Retrieved from: https://www.ncbi.nlm.nih.gov/pubmed/27333231

Buford, G. (2016) *Eat, Drink, Heal.* Createspace.

Can Vitamin D Tame Fibrosis? (2013 July 5). Retrieved from: https://www.hopkinsmedicine.org/news/publications/inside_tract/inside_tract_spring_2013/can_vitamin_d_tame_fibrosis

Cleavers (2015, May 23). Retrieved from: https://wa.kaiserpermanente.org/kbase/topic.jhtml?docId=hn-2070002

Croft KD, Codde JP, Barden A, Vandongen R, & Beilin LJ. Effect of dietary fish oils on the formation of leukotriene B4 and B5, thromboxane and platelet activating factor by rat leukocytes. *Clin Exp Pharmacol Physiol.* 1988;15(7):517–525. doi:10.1111/j.1440-1681.1988.tb01109.x Retrieved from: https://pubmed.ncbi.nlm.nih.gov/2856061/

Cross, M., Yi, P., Thomas, C., Garcia, J. &Valle, C. (2014). Evaluation of Malnutrition in Orthopaedic Surgery. The Journal of the American Academy of Orthopaedic Surgeons. 22. 193-9. 10.5435/JAAOS-22-03-193. Retrieved from: https://insights.ovid.com/american-academy-orthopaedic-surgeons/jaaos/2014/03/000/evaluation-malnutrition-orthopaedic-surgery/7/00124635

de Castro, S. M. M., van den Esschert, J. W., van Heek, N. T., Dalhuisen, S., Koelemay, M. J. W., Busch, O. R. C., & Gouma, D. J. (2008). A systematic review of the efficacy of gum chewing for the amelioration of postoperative ileus. *Digestive Surgery*, 2008(25), 39–45. doi: 10.1159/000117822. Retrieved from: https://link.springer.com/article/10.1007/s12070-014-0814-3?shared-article-renderer

Fang, F., Liu, L., Yang, Y., Tamaki, Z., Wei, J., Marangoni, R. G., Bhattacharyya, S., Summer, R. S., Ye, B., & Varga, J. (2012). The adipokine adiponectin has potent anti-fibrotic effects mediated via adenosine monophosphate-activated protein kinase: novel target for fibrosis therapy. *Arthritis research & therapy, 14*(5), R229. https://doi.org/10.1186/ar4070 Retrieved from: https://www.ncbi.nlm.nih.gov/pmc/articles/PMC3580540/

Földi E, Földi M, (eds) (2012) Textbook of lymphology. Munich: Urban and Fischer.

Gkegkes I, D, Minis E, E, & Iavazzo C: Effect of Caffeine Intake on Postoperative Ileus: A Systematic Review and Meta-Analysis. Dig Surg 2019. doi: 10.1159/000496431 Retrieved from: https://www.karger.com/Article/FullText/496431#

Gómez-Ramírez S, Bisbe E, Shander A, Spahn D, R, & Muñoz M: Management of Perioperative Iron Deficiency Anemia. Acta Haematol 2019;142:21-29. doi: 10.1159/000496965 Retrieved from: https://www.karger.com/Article/FullText/496965#

Grass, G., Rensing, C., & Solioz, M. (2011). Metallic copper as an antimicrobial surface. *Applied and environmental microbiology, 77*(5), 1541–1547. doi:10.1128/AEM.02766-10 Retrieved from: https://www.ncbi.nlm.nih.gov/pmc/articles/PMC3067274/

Harvard Health Letter. Gut reaction: A limited role for digestive enzyme supplements. Last updated Jan 29, 2020. Accessed Apr 2, 2020 https://www.health.harvard.edu/staying-healthy/gut-reaction-a-limited-role-for-digestive-enzyme-supplements

Herrera, J., Henke, C. A., & Bitterman, P. B. (2018). Extracellular matrix as a driver of progressive fibrosis. *The Journal of clinical investigation, 128*(1), 45–53. https://doi.org/10.1172/JCI93557. Retrieved from: https://www.ncbi.nlm.nih.gov/pmc/articles/PMC5749528/

Herzig, S., & Shaw, R. J. (2018). AMPK: guardian of metabolism and mitochondrial homeostasis. *Nature reviews. Molecular cell biology, 19*(2), 121–135. https://doi.org/10.1038/nrm.2017.95 Retrieved from: https://www.ncbi.nlm.nih.gov/pmc/articles/PMC5780224/

Izadi, V., & Azadbakht, L. (2015). Specific dietary patterns and concentrations of adiponectin. *Journal of research in medical sciences : the official journal of Isfahan University of Medical Sciences, 20*(2), 178–184. Retrieved from: https://www.ncbi.nlm.nih.gov/pmc/articles/PMC4400715/

Jamshidi, N. & Cohen, M. M. (2017). The Clinical Efficacy and Safety of Tulsi in Humans: A Systematic Review of the Literature. *Evidence-based complementary and alternative medicine: eCAM, 2017*, 9217567. doi:10.1155/2017/9217567. Retrieved from: https://www.ncbi.nlm.

nih.gov/pmc/articles/PMC5376420/pdf/ECAM2017-9217567.pdf

Illiano, P., Brambilla, R. & Parolini, C. (2020). The mutual interplay of gut microbiota, diet and human disease. The FEBS Journal. 10.1111/febs.15217. Retrieved from: https://febs.onlinelibrary.wiley.com/doi/full/10.1111/febs.15217

Jiang, S., Li, T., Yang, Z., Yi, W., Di, S., and Sun, Y., & Wang, D. (2017). AMPK orchestrates an elaborate cascade protecting tissue from fibrosis and aging. Ageing Research Reviews. 38. 10.1016/j.arr.2017.07.001. Retrieved from: https://www.ncbi.nlm.nih.gov/pubmed/28709692

Kaufman, C. (2020 January 23). Foods to Fight Iron Deficiency. Retrieved from: https://www.eatright.org/health/wellness/preventing-illness/iron-deficiency

Kaur, L., & Boland, M. (2013). Influence of kiwifruit on protein digestion. *Advances in food and nutrition research, 68*, 149-67 . Retrieved from: https://www.sciencedirect.com/science/article/pii/B9780123942944000080?via%3Dihub

Kim, J., Yang, G., Kim, Y., Kim, J., & Ha, J. (2016). AMPK activators: mechanisms of action and physiological activities. *Experimental & molecular medicine, 48*(4), e224. https://doi.org/10.1038/emm.2016.16 Retrieved from: https://www.ncbi.nlm.nih.gov/pmc/articles/PMC4855276/

Kim, T., Davis, J., Zhang, J., He, X. & Mathews, S. (2009). Curcumin activates AMPK and suppresses gluconeogenic gene expression in hepatoma cells. Biochemical and biophysical research communications. 388. 377-82. 10.1016/j.bbrc.2009.08.018. Retrieved from: https://www.researchgate.net/publication/26727874_Curcumin_activates_AMPK_and_suppresses_gluconeogenic_gene_expression_in_hepatoma_cells

Kunnumakkara, A. B., Sailo, B. L., Banik, K., Harsha, C., Prasad, S., Gupta, S. C., & Aggarwal, B. B. (2018). Chronic diseases, inflammation, and spices: how are they linked? *Journal of translational medicine, 16*(1), 14. doi:10.1186/s12967-018-1381-2 Retrieved from: https://

www.ncbi.nlm.nih.gov/pmc/articles/PMC5785894/

Lai X, -F, Qin H, -D, Guo L, -L, Luo Z, -G, Chang J, & Qin C, -C: Hypercholesterolemia Increases the Production of Leukotriene B4 in Neutrophils by Enhancing the Nuclear Localization of 5-Lipoxygenase. Cell Physiol Biochem 2014;34:1723-1732. doi: 10.1159/000366373. Retrieved from: https://www.karger.com/Article/Fulltext/366373

Laidlaw, T. (2012). Low fat diet with fish oils can reduce LTB4 levels. Retrieved from: https://aerd.partners.org/low-fat-diet-with-fish-oils-can-reduce-ltb4-levels/

Lavender. See "NCCIH."

Liu, S. H., Chiu, C. Y., Wang, L. P., & Chiang, M. T. (2019). Omega-3 Fatty Acids-Enriched Fish Oil Activates AMPK/PGC-1α Signaling and Prevents Obesity-Related Skeletal Muscle Wasting. *Marine drugs, 17*(6), 380. https://doi.org/10.3390/md17060380 Retrieved from: https://www.ncbi.nlm.nih.gov/pmc/articles/PMC6628302/

Lytvyn, L., Quach, K., Banfield, L., Johnston, B.C. & Mertz, D. (2015). Probiotics and synbiotics for the prevention of postoperative infections following abdominal surgery: A systematic review and meta-analysis of randomized controlled trials. *Journal of Hospital Infection*. 92. 10.1016/j.jhin.2015.08.028. Retrieved from: https://www.researchgate.net/publication/284018738_Probiotics_and_synbiotics_for_the_prevention_of_postoperative_infections_following_abdominal_surgery_A_systematic_review_and_meta-analysis_of_randomized_controlled_trials

MacKay, D. & Miller, A. L. (2003). Nutritional support for wound healing. *Alternative Medicine Review, 8*(4), 359–377. Retrieved from http://archive.foundationalmedicinereview.com/publications/8/4/359.pdf.

Markowiak, P., & Śliżewska, K. (2017). Effects of Probiotics, Prebiotics, and Synbiotics on Human Health. *Nutrients, 9*(9), 1021. https://doi.org/10.3390/nu9091021. Retrieved from: https://www.ncbi.nlm.nih.gov/pmc/articles/PMC5622781/

McCaffrey, J. (2011) Eat to Heal. Createspace.

McKay, D. & Blumberg, J. (2006). A Review of the bioactivity and potential health benefits of peppermint tea (Mentha piperita L). Phytotherapy Research. 20. 619-633. 10.1002/ptr.1936. Retrieved from: https://www.ncbi.nlm.nih.gov/pubmed/16767798

Mine, Y., Wong, A. & Jiang, B. (2005). Fibrinolytic enzymes in Asian traditional fermented foods. Food Research International. 38. 243-250. 10.1016/j.foodres.2004.04.008. Retrieved from: https://www.sciencedirect.com/science/article/abs/pii/S096399690400242X

Muhammad ZA, & Ahmad T. Therapeutic uses of pineapple-extracted bromelain in surgical care–A review. J Pak Med Assoc. 2017;67(1):121-125.Retrieved from: https://pubmed.ncbi.nlm.nih.gov/28065968/

Muss, C., Mosgoeller, W., & Endler, T. (2013). Papaya preparation (Caricol®) in digestive disorders. Neuro endocrinology letters, 34 1, 38-46 . Retrieved from: https://www.ncbi.nlm.nih.gov/pubmed/23524622

Nanda MS & Kaur M. Role of Oral enzymes in post-operative septoplasty Cases. Indian J Otolaryngol Head Neck Surg 2019 Nov; 71;(Suppl 3): 1663-1667.

NCCIH. (2016 Nov. 30). Lavender. Retrieved from https://nccih.nih.gov/health/lavender/ataglance.htm

Orsini, Roger. (2007). Bromelain. Plastic and reconstructive surgery. 118. 1640-4. 10.1097/01.prs.0000242503.50548.ee. Retrieved from: https://www.researchgate.net/publication/6694400_Bromelain

Patra, J. K., Das, G., Paramithiotis, S., & Shin, H. S. (2016). Kimchi and Other Widely Consumed Traditional Fermented Foods of Korea: A Review. *Frontiers in microbiology, 7*, 1493. https://doi.org/10.3389/fmicb.2016.01493 Retrieved from: https://www.ncbi.nlm.nih.gov/pmc/articles/PMC5039233/

Proteolytic Enzymes. (2019, May 17). Retrieved from: https://www.mskcc.org/cancer-care/integrative-medicine/herbs/proteolytic-enzymes

Quain, A. & Khardori, N. (2015). Nutrition in Wound Care Management: A Comprehensive Overview. Wounds : a compendium of clinical research and practice. 27. 327-335. Retrieved from: https://www.woundsresearch.com/article/nutrition-wound-care-management-comprehensive-overview

Raveendran, S., Parameswaran, B., Ummalyma, S. B., Abraham, A., Mathew, A. K., Madhavan, A., … Pandey, A. (2018). Applications of Microbial Enzymes in Food Industry. *Food technology and biotechnology, 56*(1), 16–30. doi:10.17113/ftb.56.01.18.5491 Retrieved from: https://www.ncbi.nlm.nih.gov/pmc/articles/PMC5956270/

Red Clover (2015 March 24). Retrieved from: http://pennstatehershey.adam.com/content.aspx?productid=107&pid=33&gid=000270

Richter, E. A. & Ruderman, N. B. (2009). AMPK and the biochemistry of exercise: implications for human health and disease. *The Biochemical journal, 418*(2), 261–275. https://doi.org/10.1042/BJ20082055 Retrieved from: https://www.ncbi.nlm.nih.gov/pmc/articles/PMC2779044/#R24

Roy, M., Perry, J. & Cross, Karen. (2018). Nutrition and the Plastic Surgeon: Possible Interventions and Practice Considerations. Plastic and Reconstructive Surgery–Global Open. Latest Articles. 1. 10.1097/GOX.0000000000001704. Retrieved from: https://journals.lww.com/prsgo/Fulltext/2018/08000/Nutrition_and_the_Plastic_Surgeon_Possible.23.aspx

Scallan, C. (2003). *Herbal cures: Healing remedies from Ireland.* Dublin: Newleaf.

Simonson W. (2019). Should vitamin C routinely be given with oral iron supplements? *Geriatric nursing (New York, N.Y.), 40*(3), 327–328. https://doi.org/10.1016/j.gerinurse.2019.05.007 Retrieved from: https://www.sciencedirect.com/science/article/pii/S0197457219302599?via%3Dihub

Siva, N., Johnson, C.R., Richard, V.L., Jesch, E., Whiteside, W.S., Abood, A.A., Thavarajah, P., Duckett, S.K., & Thavarajah, D. (2018). Lentil ( Lens culinaris Medikus) Diet Affects the Gut Microbiome and Obesity Markers in Rat. *Journal of agricultural and food chemistry, 66 33*, 8805-8813 . Retrieved from: https://pubmed.ncbi.nlm.nih.gov/30102041-lentil-lens-culinaris-medikus-diet-affects-the-gut-microbiome-and-obesity-markers-in-rat/?from_term=lentil&from_pos=1

Stephani, L., Tjandrawinata, R., Afifah, D., Lim, Y., Ismaya, W. & Suhartono, M. (2017). Food Origin Fibrinolytic Enzyme With Multiple Actions. HAYATI Journal of Biosciences. 24. 10.1016/j.hjb.2017.09.003. Retrieved from: https://www.sciencedirect.com/science/article/pii/S1978301917301432

Tian W, Rockson SG, Jiang X, et al. Leukotriene B4 antagonism ameliorates experimental lymphedema. *Sci Transl Med.* 2017;9(389):eaal3920. doi:10.1126/scitranslmed.aal3920 Retrieved from: https://pubmed.ncbi.nlm.nih.gov/28490670/

Torres, E. C., & Sawyer, T. L. (2006). *Healing with Herbs and Rituals a Mexican Tradition*. Albuquerque: University of New Mexico Press.

Varayil, J., Bauer, B. & Hurt R. (2014) Over-the-Counter Enzyme Supplements: What a Clinician Needs to Know. Retrieved from: https://www.mayoclinicproceedings.org/article/S0025-6196(14)00520-5/pdf

Weng, Y., Yao, J., Sparks, S., & Wang, K. Y. (2017). Nattokinase: An Oral Antithrombotic Agent for the Prevention of Cardiovascular Disease. *International journal of molecular sciences, 18*(3), 523. doi:10.3390/ijms18030523 Retrieved from: https://www.ncbi.nlm.nih.gov/pmc/articles/PMC5372539/

Wischmeyer, P., Carli, F., Evans, D., Guilbert, S., Kozar, R., Pryor, A., Thiele, R., Everett, S., Grocott, M., Gan, T., Shaw, A., Thacker, J., Miller, T., Hedrick, T., Mcevoy, M., Mythen, G., Bergamaschi, R., Gupta, R., Holubar, S. & Fiore Jr, J. (2018). American Society for Enhanced Recovery and Perioperative Quality Initiative Joint Consensus Statement on Nutrition Screening and Therapy Within a Surgical

Enhanced Recovery Pathway. Anesthesia & Analgesia. 126. 1. 10.1213/ANE.0000000000002743. Retrieved from: https://journals.lww.com/anesthesia-analgesia/fulltext/2018/06000/american_society_for_enhanced_recovery_and.19.aspx

Yarnell, E. & Abascal, K. (2013). Antifibrotic Herbs: Indications, Mechanisms of Action, Doses, and Safety Information. Alternative and Complementary Therapies. 19. 75-82. 10.1089/act.2013.19203. Retrieved from: https://www.researchgate.net/publication/275200316_Antifibrotic_Herbs_Indications_Mechanisms_of_Action_Doses_and_Safety_Information

Yuan, Y., Das, S. K., & Li, M. (2018). Vitamin D ameliorates impaired wound healing in streptozotocin-induced diabetic mice by suppressing NF-κB-mediated inflammatory genes. *Bioscience reports, 38*(2), BSR20171294. https://doi.org/10.1042/BSR20171294. Retrieved from: https://www.ncbi.nlm.nih.gov/pmc/articles/PMC5835716/